dream desserts

LUSCIOUS, LOW-FAT RECIPES

Chocolate Soufflé *(recipe on pages 78–79)*

dream desserts
LUSCIOUS, LOW-FAT RECIPES

NANCY BAGGETT

Photographs by Martin Jacobs

STEWART, TABORI & CHANG
NEW YORK

Text © 1993 Nancy Baggett
Photographs © 1993 Martin Jacobs

Published in 1993 by
Stewart, Tabori & Chang, Inc.
575 Broadway, New York, New York 10012

Library of Congress Cataloging-in-Publication Data
Baggett, Nancy, 1943–
Dream desserts : luscious, low-fat recipes /
by Nancy Baggett ; photographs by Martin Jacobs.
p.   cm.
ISBN 1-55670-273-6 : $24.95
1. Low-fat diet—Recipes. 2. Low-calorie diet—Recipes.
3. Low-cholesterol diet—Recipes. 4. Desserts. I. Title.
RM237 . 7 . B34   1993
641.8'6—dc20   92-37781

Distributed in the U.S. by Workman Publishing,
708 Broadway, New York, New York 10003
Distributed in Canada by Canadian Manda Group,
P.O. Box 920 Station U, Toronto, Ontario M8Z 5P9
Distributed in all other territories (except Central
and South America) by Melia Publishing Services,
P.O. Box 1639, Maidenhead, Berkshire SL6 6YZ England
Central and South American accounts should contact
Export Sales Manager, Stewart, Tabori & Chang.

Printed in Japan
10 9 8 7 6 5 4 3 2 1

acknowledgments

Many thanks go to publisher Leslie Stoker and editor Andrea Danese for their great enthusiasm and support for this project. Also, thanks to the book's designer, Amanda Wilson, to copy editor Melanie Falick, and to the entire Stewart, Tabori & Chang staff for their professionalism and good will.

I am indebted to the extraordinary team who worked with me on the photographs for *Dream Desserts*. Food stylist Deborah Mintcheff and prop stylist Linda Johnson contributed tremendous professional expertise and creative energy. Photographer Marty Jacobs worked sheer magic, transforming food, light, color, and design into breath-taking art.

Thanks to Mike Dalgleish, who assisted in my kitchen with great efficiency and good humor, and to Margaret Menard and Judy Benson, who also assisted me. Denise Donohue and Arlene Swantko carefully and enthusiastically home-tested the recipes.

Finally, deepest thanks go to my agent Linda Hayes for her wisdom, friendship, and support on this and every project.

AND ORANG

contents

Opposite: Nana's Orange Sponge Cake *(recipe on pages 24–25)*

introduction

For many years the idea of being able to eat truly tempting, luxurious desserts without feeling guilty struck me as a fantasy. Except for sorbets and simple fruit dishes, the low-fat or "diet" desserts I sampled were always long on diet and short on the pleasure that is—or should be—inherent in the word dessert. Concoctions like tofu cheesecake, fat- and sugar-free whole wheat–honey cake, and gelatin fluffs topped with evaporated milk "whipped cream" ranked among the worst of the strange "goodies" I tried.

My simple rule on desserts, low-fat or otherwise, has always been that if they don't taste and look *really wonderful,* they are not worth wasting calories or fat on, and are certainly not worth making! Food is not medicine, as Julia Child has so aptly noted, and perhaps more than any other fare, dessert should be enjoyed, not prescribed.

This is not to say I reject the value of either healthful eating or nutritionally improved recipes. In fact, as far back as fifteen years ago I started reducing fat in my own home-cooking, and in 1984 I coauthored a cookbook, *Don't Tell 'Em It's Good for 'Em,* that was a Tastemaker Award finalist for best book in the health and diet category. However, I have never been willing to compromise on appeal, and particularly in the case of desserts, low-fat and thoroughly satisfying often seemed to be a contradiction in terms. My approach was to stick to a prudent daily regime that allowed for occasional sweet indulgences. And when I did indulge, I wanted desserts so sublime they were absolutely, positively worth saving up for.

During the last eight years, I have devoted a lot of time to creating great desserts. I spent a year studying with White House Executive Pastry Chef Roland Mesnier, and also wrote *The International Cookie Cookbook* in 1988 and *The International Chocolate Cookbook* in 1991. At the same time, I began applying techniques for reducing fat to my dessert making. First came a book on baking with oat bran, then several articles on light desserts and baked goods for *Eating Well* magazine.

The response to my recipes in *Eating Well* was so enthusiastic that I began to believe that it might be possible to create a whole book of low- and reduced-fat sweets that delivered the enjoyment every dessert should. Perhaps I could fulfill the ultimate food fantasy—a full complement of luscious indulgences, including cakes, pies, cookies, brownies, puddings, and mousses, that would meet the expectations of even the most discriminating dessert lovers, but would also fit comfortably into a healthful eating regime.

That was what I proposed to my publisher, though in truth the task seemed daunting. To make sure the desserts really were delectable, I took a few precautions. Every recipe in *Dream Desserts* was assessed by numerous tasters, and the questions I always asked included: "If you didn't know this was reduced in fat, could you tell?" And, "Would you rate this highly if you thought it was a 'regular' dessert?" Anything that elicited the it's-good-for-a-diet-recipe response was jettisoned from the book. The last creation voted down was—alas—a cheesecake, which my tasters happily agreed was good enough to warrant seconds, but might be recognized as "health food." (Not to worry, though. There is a reduced-fat cheesecake in this book that received very high grades!)

To ensure that the recipes really were nutritionally improved, I resolved that each would be analyzed for calories, fat, saturated fat, cholesterol, and sodium, as well as for the total percentage of calories from fat. (This last figure is particularly useful, since experts now say that 30 percent or fewer total calories

from fat is a prudent daily target; see page 12 for details.) Moreover, I promised myself not to play games with the numbers. For example, I would not artificially reduce the grams of fat per serving by suggesting that a standard-size layer cake or cheesecake would yield 24 slices! Portion sizes would reflect the way the average person eats. To the same end, I vowed to take into account the way people really cook. While a pastry chef might be able to scrimp on pie crust by rolling it paper-thin (thereby reducing fat and cholesterol), most home cooks would find this a frustrating task.

Since I wanted to appeal to both those who must restrict fat intake and those who are just looking to lighten up where possible, the book includes a wide variety of fat-free and low-fat sweets (low-fat sweets are defined as those containing 5 grams of fat or less per serving), as well as many reduced-fat recipes (those that are not quite low enough in fat to fit into the low-fat category, but are significantly less fatty than their traditional counterparts). Among the most remarkable of these are delicious, fudgy brownies that slash *total fat by half and saturated fat and cholesterol to almost zero* and a moist, buttery pound cake that reduces *total fat by almost two-thirds and saturated fat by nearly three-fourths.* Even more impressive is a tempting, creamy-rich cheesecake *with about one-fourth the fat of a conventional one:* My "improved" version has 9.25 grams of fat per slice compared to 35 grams a slice for regular cheesecake. (See page 13 for a direct comparison.)

How was it possible to achieve such dramatic reductions without affecting flavor? "Very carefully!" is the glib answer. With some of the same easy but little-known tricks and techniques pastry chefs and other very experienced cooks use to make desserts taste wonderful is the more illuminating response. Sometimes I even call for the same rich ingredients that most chefs depend on, though I use them in *much smaller quantities* and less frequently. I've found it simply does not work to banish all egg yolks, butter, cream, cream cheese, nuts, and chocolate from all recipes. For authentic custard flavor, you need some egg yolk; for butteriness, a bit of real butter; for cream cheese taste, a little reduced-fat cream cheese. However, the amount of these ingredients required to create the illusion of lushness is often so small that the nutritional counts are actually better than if larger amounts of synthetic this or substitute that were used. But even more important, a tablespoon of cream or a single egg yolk can sometimes mean the difference between a reduced-fat and -cholesterol dessert that people will make and enjoy for a lifetime, and a "treat" that only desperate dieters or devoted health foodies could love.

With *Dream Desserts* I set out to prove that it is possible to strike a balance between the demands of health and pleasures of eating. That we can eat sensibly without having to give up one of our favorite indulgences, dessert. Frankly, the recipes here exceeded my expectations, being at once more healthful and more truly enticing than I'd hoped. Enjoy them in good health.

About Making Low-Fat Desserts

*T*t's easy to summarize my attitude about eating healthfully: I want to have my cake and eat it too. Of course, I'd like to pare fat, cholesterol, and extra calories from my diet, but I don't want to give up any of the pleasures of food. And I absolutely cannot imagine doing without wonderful desserts.

My belief that most of us will eat an occasional brownie or slice of cheesecake, and that this eventuality should be planned for, was one of the basic premises behind the creation of this book. Though it might make perfect sense, from a health standpoint, to eliminate sweets altogether, only the most determined among us could ever stick to such a grim, abstemious regime. Another basic premise of this book was that simply calling something that is sweet "dessert" doesn't make it satisfying. Desserts, especially nutritionally improved ones, must at least seem like indulgences, or we will simply bypass them for something that delivers real satisfaction—and probably more fat, cholesterol, and calories.

In the following pages, the nutritional underpinnings of *Dream Desserts* are explained. Despite all the details and numbers given, remember that my first consideration when creating a new dessert was always taste. It did not matter if a recipe was terrific from a nutritional point of view. If it wasn't delicious I didn't include it in this book.

How Low Is Low-Fat?

Dream Desserts includes some recipes that are low-fat and low-cholesterol and some that are reduced-fat and reduced-cholesterol. To decide how lean recipes needed to be to warrant labeling them "low-fat" or "low-cholesterol," I relied on current nutritional recommendations and common sense. Most dietary guidelines suggest that daily fat intake should be limited to 30 percent or less of total calories. Of course, not every dish must comply with this 30-percent rule as long as no more than 30 percent of the day's total calories come from fat. Many guidelines go on to suggest *maximum daily limits* of 50 to 65 grams of total fat, no more than a third of which is saturated, and 250 to 300 milligrams of cholesterol. (The exact limits depend on individual calorie intake and body size.)

Keeping in mind that desserts are usually among the richer menu items and that many people prefer to trim fat in other parts of their diet to accommodate a satisfying dessert, I did not try to cut out virtually all fat; instead, I set a ceiling for low-fat and low-cholesterol recipes of 5 grams of fat and 30 milligrams of cholesterol, roughly one tenth of the daily total. I also aimed to keep total calories from fat under 30 percent, a goal that nearly all the recipes in this book easily meet. (A very large share, in fact, derive only 10 to 25 percent of their calories from fat, and there are some that have an even lower percentage of fat.)

Most of the "reduced-fat" or "reduced-cholesterol" recipes contain less than 10 grams of fat and 60 milligrams of cholesterol per serving and also offer significant nutritional improvements over the original desserts. To check myself, I frequently compared my "improved" desserts with their ordinary counterparts.

In the case of pound cake, for example, many standard recipes call for 3 or 4 whole eggs, a cup (sometimes much more) of butter, and a cup of sour cream, yielding 12 servings with about 20 grams of fat and more than 125 milligrams of cholesterol each. In contrast, in the moist, buttery-tasting pound cake on pages 28–29, the sour cream is replaced with nonfat yogurt, and the recipe calls for only ¼ cup of butter, 2 ½ tablespoons of low-saturated-fat vegetable oil, and 1 whole egg—yielding 12 servings with 7.3 grams of fat and 28 milligrams of cholesterol each. There is an even more striking contrast between the fat and cholesterol contents of the *Dream Desserts* Deli-Style Lemon Cheesecake (pages 54–56) and traditional cheesecake, as the side-by-side comparison of the two ingredient lists reveals. The *Dream Desserts* version weighs in at a respectable 9.25 grams of fat and 62 milligrams of cholesterol. The unimproved cheesecake of the same size and type has a staggering 35 grams of fat and 202 milligrams of cholesterol (nearly two-thirds of the recommended daily total!).

I did not set specific goals for lowering calories in *Dream Desserts,* but to accommodate today's taste for less sweet desserts, sugar was always used judiciously.

Moreover, reductions in fat automatically meant dramatic reductions in calories, since fats are twice as calorie dense as other ingredients. All fats contain 9 calories per gram, compared to 4 calories per gram for all starches, sugars, and proteins. This explains why my cheesecake not only has less fat than the traditional one, but also has about 250 fewer calories per serving.

About the Nutritional Analysis

All recipes and variations have been professionally analyzed to provide the percentage of calories from fat, as well as total calories, fat, saturated fat, choles-

Dream Desserts
Deli-Style Lemon Cheesecake

Crumb Crust
Generous ³⁄₄ cup graham cracker crumbs
1 tablespoon chilled unsalted butter
¹⁄₂ tablespoon light corn syrup

Filling
1 cup plain, *additive-free* nonfat yogurt (see Note)
Scant 1 cup granulated sugar
Finely grated zest (yellow part of skin) of 1 large lemon
2 large eggs plus 4 large egg whites
2 teaspoons fresh lemon juice
2¹⁄₂ teaspoons vanilla extract
2 cups 1-percent fat, salt-free cottage cheese
12 ounces reduced-fat cream cheese (sometimes called Neufchâtel cheese), cut into chunks and at room temperature
¹⁄₄ cup all-purpose flour

Makes 12 servings.

Per serving (based on 12 servings):
Calories: 223   Grams of fat: 9.25   Grams of saturated fat: 5.3
Mgrams cholesterol: 62   Mgrams sodium: 267
Percentage of calories from fat: 37

Traditional (Unimproved)
Deli-Style Cheesecake

Crumb Crust
1¹⁄₄ cups graham cracker crumbs
¹⁄₄ cup unsalted butter, melted
1 tablespoon granulated sugar

Filling
1¹⁄₄ cups granulated sugar
4 (8-ounce) packages cream cheese, cut into chunks and at room temperature
4 large eggs
2 large egg yolks
¹⁄₄ cup sour cream
Finely grated zest of 1 medium lemon
2 tablespoons fresh lemon juice
2 teaspoons vanilla extract

Makes 12 servings.

Per serving (based on 12 servings):
Calories: 475   Grams of fat: 35   Grams of saturated fat: 22
Mgrams cholesterol: 202   Mgrams sodium: 307
Percentage of calories from fat: 65

terol, and sodium *per serving*. Note that where a range of servings is given the analysis is based on the larger number. Every effort has been made to divide desserts into realistic portion sizes so that the nutritional analyses reflect actual, not ideal intake.

In recipes where a choice of several ingredients or a range in the quantity of an ingredient is given, the nutritional analysis is based on the first entry. In instances where toppings or garnishes are optional, there are separate analyses showing the dish with and without the optional item.

On Low-Fat Dessert-Making

If there is one key to creating truly tempting low-fat desserts, it is moderation. It really doesn't work to completely ban all fatty ingredients, nor does it work to go overboard with the "skinny" ones. Though one's first impulse is often to forbid such fatty items as butter, egg yolks, cream, and chocolate, I have found that, from both a taste and nutrition standpoint, desserts usually come out better if very small amounts of these ingredients are used when necessary. Sometimes, in trying to duplicate the flavor and texture of these ingredients with substitutes you actually add more fat, cholesterol, and calories than you would have added by simply using the real thing judiciously. Other times, the desserts made with substitutes simply taste so disappointing that they no longer seem like desserts. By the same token, if you toss in too much of a "healthy" ingredient like powdered milk or non-fat yogurt, you can end up with a dessert that has a leaden texture and an unappetizing taste.

Almost without exception, the ingredients called for in *Dream Desserts* are the same ones used in traditional dessert-making. However, some are used more or less frequently or in a slightly different way than in traditional recipes, as described below.

Butter In this book butter is only used as a flavor enhancer, not to provide all the fat a recipe needs. Butter, regular stick margarine, and vegetable oils all have approximately the same amount of fat per tablespoon, 11 to 12 grams, so choosing one or another does not have a substantial effect on the overall amount of fat in a dessert. However, butter does have much more saturated fat than the low-saturated-fat vegetable oils, such as canola, safflower, and corn oils, so this needs to be taken into account. Often, to obtain fine, buttery flavor and still hold the saturated fat count down to under a third of the total, I call for both butter and oil in recipes. A little butter goes a long way, but to get the absolute most flavor possible, I sometimes brown it (see recipe, page 147), which heightens the rich taste and aroma even further. Low-saturated-fat vegetable oils work well to prevent dryness and toughness in recipes but contribute nothing to a dessert's taste.

The choice between butter or margarine is complicated by the fact that some margarines are higher in saturated fat than others. The "diet" tub-style spreads and "light" stick margarines, which are often the lowest in saturated fat, cannot be directly compared to butter because they contain a lot of water and sometimes a lot of air. (The water also renders them unsuitable for some cooked dishes and baked goods, especially cookies and pastries.) Regular stick margarines, which can be directly compared to butter, generally have 2 or 3 grams of saturated fat per tablespoon versus 7 grams per tablespoon for butter. However, the stick margarines contain trans-fatty acids, fats that while not saturated have the same cholesterol-raising effects on the body as saturated fats. Considering the great flavor advantage of butter and the fact that tiny amounts will suffice, I prefer to use it in combination with oil rather than rely on margarine. Should you prefer margarine, you simply substitute it for the unsalted butter called for in the recipes in this book, but be aware that it cannot be browned to enhance flavor.

Citrus Zest This is the colored part of the skin of fresh lemons, oranges, and other citrus fruit. Adding zest is one of the best ways to boost the flavor in recipes that might otherwise seem lacking when excess fat is pared away. Citrus zest enlivens fruit compotes, sauces, and baked goods, especially those containing molasses, spice, or fruit. Shredded and candied zest also adds appealing color and textural interest to desserts. Since zest is fat-free, it can be used as abundantly as desired.

When grating or peeling away citrus zest, take care not to remove the white layer of pith underneath; it tastes bitter.

Eggs Egg whites and yolks arrive together in a tidy natural package, but serve different purposes in dessert-making and must be considered as separate ingredients when trying to reduce fat and cholesterol. Whites are virtually fat and cholesterol free, while large yolks have 5 grams of fat (1.5 grams of it saturated) and 215 milligrams of cholesterol apiece.

Egg whites serve a number of important functions in desserts: from binding ingredients together in cookies and some cakes; to providing lightness and volume in soufflés, puffy baked puddings, and sponge cakes; to producing fat-free pastry meringue shells and crisp layers for tortes and dacquoises.

In the past, uncooked beaten egg whites were also a convenient, fat-free way to fluff mousses, bavarians, and meringue toppings and frostings. Now that food handling guidelines dictate that all eggs must be cooked, such recipes have to be eliminated or modified. Meringue pie toppings, for example, now must be fully baked rather than briefly browned under a broiler. To make it possible to safely use egg whites in fluffy frostings, mousses, and unbaked soufflés, I have revised the traditional method for preparing Italian meringue (a classic pastry technique in which hot sugar syrup is gradually beaten into whites). In the revised process (pages 150–51), the syrup is made hot enough and added to the whites fast enough to raise their temperature to about 160° F. and then hold their temperature above 140° F. for about 3 minutes, which ensures that the whites cook fully and are safe to eat.

Since egg yolks are a bit fatty and are high in cholesterol, they should only be used when truly necessary—for instance, to promote tenderness in baked goods or to impart the appealing eggy taste and color in custards, puddings and creamy fillings. Fortunately, it doesn't usually take a lot of egg yolk to lend rich creamy flavor.

In cases when whole eggs are added in traditional recipes to bind ingredients together (in many quick bread doughs and cookies, for example), the yolks can simply be omitted because it is the whites that do most of the binding. It isn't desirable to replace the yolks with extra whites because excess whites can make baked goods rubbery and dry.

Liquid egg substitutes can sometimes be used instead of eggs, though I greatly prefer to simply call for either whites or yolks, as needed. It is particularly advantageous nutritionally when only whites are required because whites have less sodium than egg substitutes and no gums, stabilizers, or other additives. Moreover, some brands of liquid egg substitutes (but not all) contain fat (up to 2 grams per "egg") and thus add fat while whites used alone do not.

Chocolate and Cocoa Like egg whites and yolks, chocolate and unsweetened cocoa powder, both of which come from cocoa beans, are natural companions. However, while cocoa powder (the powder that remains when most of the cocoa butter is pressed from unsweetened chocolate) contains only about 1 gram of fat per tablespoon and is, therefore, an easy, low-fat way to lend chocolatey flavor to cakes and other baked goods, 1 ounce of unsweetened chocolate contains about 15 grams of fat and must be used more carefully. Nevertheless, I like to add a little chocolate to chocolate sauces, fillings, and frostings because it lends a rounder, richer taste than cocoa alone. To compensate for the extra fat contributed by the chocolate, it is usually possible to trim some of the fat from other sources in the recipe.

Low-Fat Cream Cheese Also called Neufchâtel cheese, this light cream cheese is almost indistinguishable in taste and texture from regular cream cheese, but has about one third less fat. However, depending on the brand, it still has 35 to 40 grams of fat per 8-ounce package, so it cannot be used with abandon.

Note that the recipes in this book call for *packages* of Neufchâtel cheese, *not* tub-style Neufchâtel cheese "spread." The spread has a higher water content and will not yield satisfactory results.

Nonfat Dry Milk To reduce overall fat content, whipped nonfat dry milk can sometimes be substituted for whipped cream in mousses, chiffon pies, and other unbaked, aerated desserts. It works best with citrus and other zesty mixtures that balance its slightly over-sweet taste. To ensure good results, use only top-quality brands (such as Sanalac, Carnation, or others recommended for drinking), as these have a fresher, more appealing flavor.

Nuts Considering that most nuts have around 75 grams of fat per cup, it is impossible to toss many of them into a recipe and still keep it lean. Nevertheless, nuts are worth using in desserts in small quantities because of their rich, distinctive taste and appealing, crunchy texture.

To get the most flavor out of nuts, I usually toast them before incorporating them into a recipe. To stretch them even further, I often use them in the form of a praline (see recipe, pages 138–39).

Vegetable Oils Canola and safflower oil are specifically called for in this book because they have the lowest levels of saturated fats of all the readily available "flavorless" cooking oils. Canola has significant amounts of both poly- and monounsaturates, while safflower is high in polyunsaturates. Since dietary guidelines recommend that about equal amounts of poly- and monounsaturates be consumed, you might want to take the oils you are consuming in the rest of your diet into consideration when choosing which to use in the recipes in this book.

Yogurt Nonfat yogurt is one of the most useful of all dairy products in low-fat dessert making. It makes an excellent replacement for sour cream in cakes, coffee cakes, and similar doughs, contributing the same moistness and slight tanginess but without the fat. The acidity also helps tenderize baked goods, effectively countering the tendency of lean doughs to be tough from lack of fat.

In some fillings and creams, nonfat yogurt adds smoothness and welcome zest, but it must be used carefully to avoid imparting a yogurty taste. Particularly in cheesecakes, the whey must be removed from the yogurt before it is used because if it is not it will seep from the filling and make the crust soggy. When shopping for yogurt for these recipes, be sure to select a brand (such as Colombo) without gums, gelatin, starches, or other similar additives that keep the whey in suspension rather than allowing it to drain away naturally.

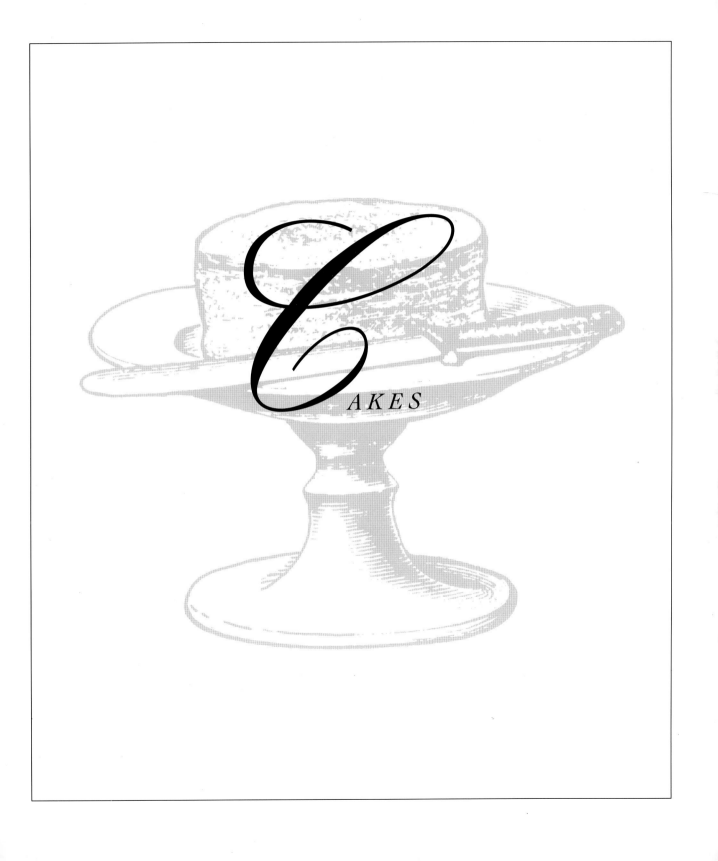

$\mathscr{C}$AKES

Chocolate Triple Layer Cake with Fluffy Chocolate Frosting

chocolate triple layer cake

A good chocolate cake always seems like an indulgence, and this one is no exception, especially when it is adorned with Fluffy Chocolate Frosting (pages 129–30). While not ultra-lean, this cake contains only 2½ tablespoons of butter and ¼ cup oil compared to a cup or more butter (and often sour cream as well) for many standard chocolate cake recipes.

1 ounce unsweetened chocolate, chopped

2 cups cake flour

6 tablespoons unsweetened American-style cocoa powder, such as Hershey's

1¾ teaspoons baking powder

½ teaspoon baking soda

¼ teaspoon salt

¼ cup canola or safflower oil

2½ tablespoons unsalted butter, slightly softened

1½ cups granulated sugar

1 large egg plus 4 large egg whites

¼ cup room-temperature coffee (or substitute water, if preferred)

2¼ teaspoons vanilla extract

¾ cup plus 2 tablespoons plain nonfat yogurt

Makes 10 to 12 servings.

Preheat oven to 350° F. Grease (or spray with non-stick spray coating) three 8- or 8½-inch round cake pans.

In a small, heavy saucepan over *lowest heat,* melt chocolate, stirring constantly until smooth; be very careful not to scorch. Set aside. Sift together flour, cocoa powder, baking powder, baking soda, and salt onto a sheet of wax paper. In a large mixer bowl, with mixer set on medium speed, beat oil, butter, and sugar until very well blended and fluffy. Beat in chocolate. One at a time, beat in egg, then whites, coffee, and vanilla, until smoothly incorporated. Gently stir half of dry ingredients, then yogurt into mixture just until mixed. Stir in remaining dry ingredients just until well blended and smooth. Divide batter among pans, spreading to edges.

Bake in middle third of oven for 23 to 28 minutes, or until tops are almost firm when tapped and a toothpick inserted in the center comes out moist but clean. Transfer pans to racks and let stand until completely cooled. Layers may be wrapped airtight and frozen for later use. Let return to room temperature before using. Or frost cake and serve immediately, if desired.

May be stored airtight for 2 or 3 days.

Per serving (based on 12 servings):
Calories: 262   Grams of fat: 9   Grams of saturated fat: 2
Mgrams cholesterol: 25   Mgrams sodium: 183
Percentage of calories from fat: 31

Per serving (with Fluffy Chocolate Frosting):
Calories: 342   Grams of fat: 10   Grams of saturated fat: 2
Mgrams cholesterol: 25   Mgrams sodium: 202
Percentage of calories from fat: 26

applesauce spice cake

A favorite of mine since childhood, this fragrant and moist homestyle cake may be served with a dusting of powdered sugar or a swirl of Fluffy Seafoam Frosting.

2 ¼ cups cake flour (unsifted)

1 ¼ teaspoons baking powder

1 teaspoon baking soda

1 ¼ teaspoons ground cinnamon

Generous ½ teaspoon ground nutmeg

Generous ½ teaspoon ground cloves

¼ teaspoon salt

⅓ cup canola or safflower oil

¾ cup granulated sugar

¾ cup packed light or dark brown sugar

1 large egg

½ teaspoon very finely grated lemon zest (yellow part of skin)

2 ½ teaspoons vanilla extract

¾ cup buttermilk

1 cup unsweetened applesauce

Sifted powdered sugar, for garnish (or Fluffy Seafoam Frosting, page 129, if preferred)

Makes 12 servings.

Preheat oven to 350° F. Grease a 10-inch tube pan, 10-cup ring pan, or 10-inch springform pan with ring inset.

Sift together flour, baking powder, baking soda, cinnamon, nutmeg, cloves, and salt onto a large sheet of wax paper. In a large mixer bowl with mixer set on medium speed, beat oil, granulated and brown sugars, egg, lemon zest, and vanilla, until well mixed and smooth. Add buttermilk and beat on low speed until incorporated. By hand, stir in about half of dry ingredients just until thoroughly incorporated. Stir in applesauce, then remaining dry ingredients; do not overmix or batter will toughen. Turn out batter into pan, lightly spreading to edges.

Bake in middle third of oven for 30 to 35 minutes or until lightly browned, center springs back when lightly pressed, and a toothpick inserted in thickest part comes out clean. (For moistest cake, do no overbake.) Transfer pan to wire rack and let stand until thoroughly cooled. Run a knife around center tube and pan sides. Invert cake onto serving plate. Frost cake top and sides with Fluffy Seafoam Frosting. Alternatively, dust cake with sifted powdered sugar just before serving.

Store cake airtight in a cool place (but not in the refrigerator) for up to 48 hours.

Per serving (based on 12 servings):
Calories: 252   Grams of fat: 6.8   Grams of saturated fat: 0.7
Mgrams cholesterol: 18   Mgrams sodium: 173
Percentage of calories from fat: 24

Per serving (with Fluffy Seafoam Frosting):
Calories: 303   Grams of fat: 6.8   Grams of saturated fat: 0.7
Mgrams cholesterol: 18   Mgrams sodium: 206
Percentage of calories from fat: 20

lemon cake roll with lemon cream & blackberry sauce

$\mathcal{L}$emon and blackberries are such a luscious combination, that they need very little added fat to taste quite rich. ⌒ In this tempting and eye-catching dessert, a light, lemon sponge cake roll is wrapped around a fragrant lemon cream and served on a pool of blackberry sauce.

1 recipe Lemon Roulade (page 144), rolled into a 10-inch-
  wide log, at room temperature or slightly cooled
⅔ cup navel orange marmalade (do not use bitter orange
  marmalade) *or* apricot preserves
1 tablespoon plus 1 teaspoon fresh lemon juice
1 recipe Lemon Filling (page 137), thoroughly cooled
¼ cup heavy (whipping) cream
Powdered sugar, for dusting cake roll
1 recipe Blackberry Sauce (page 127), chilled
1 cup fresh blackberries, for garnish (optional)

Makes 8 to 10 servings.

To ready cake roll: If lemon roulade has been refrigerated or frozen, set out to warm almost to room temperature. Combine marmalade and ½ tablespoon water in a small saucepan over medium-high heat. Bring to a simmer, stirring. Simmer for 1½ minutes and remove from heat. Stir in lemon juice. Strain marmalade through a medium-fine sieve, discarding bits of peel. Set strained mixture aside until cooled and thickened but still fluid and spreadable.

Carefully unroll roulade on a large, clean sheet of wax paper. (If surface of cake seems sticky, lightly dust the paper with powdered sugar first.) Evenly spread orange mixture over cake surface using an offset spatula or large knife. Lightly cover with wax paper and set aside while lemon cream is prepared.

To prepare lemon cream: In a mixer bowl with mixer set on high speed, beat cooled lemon filling until completely smooth. In another mixer bowl with mixer set on high speed, beat heavy cream until firm peaks form. Beat lemon filling into whipped cream until smoothly incorporated. Spread roulade surface evenly with lemon cream, stopping about 1 inch before reaching edges (to prevent filling from squeezing out during rolling). Working from a shorter side, roll up cake roll neatly (but not so tightly that cream squeezes out). Wrap tightly in wax paper, twisting ends of paper to keep it from unrolling. Transfer to a tray or baking sheet and refrigerate for at least 4 hours so flavors can mingle and up to 48 hours, if preferred.

To serve: Trim off ends of cake roll using a serrated knife. Dust length of cake roll with sifting of powdered sugar. Cut cake crosswise into slices using a sharp serrated knife and a sawing motion; cut into

1-inch slices and serve individually or cut into ½-inch slices and serve 2 per plate. Arrange slices on dessert plates and pool Blackberry Sauce around them. Garnish servings with fresh blackberries, if desired.

french-style apple upside-down cake

$\mathcal{L}$ike American pineapple upside-down cake, this recipe features a fruit layer blanketed with batter and then inverted after baking so that the fruit ends up on top. However, here the fruit is first cooked over high heat until it becomes lightly candied and browned. Though I have called this an apple cake, it is equally appealing when made with pears, so use whichever you prefer or have on hand. ∾ The recipe was inspired by a classic French dessert called Tarte Tatin.

4 to 5 Golden Delicious or Granny Smith apples, peeled, *quartered,* and cored, *or* 4 to 5 medium-sized, slightly under-ripe Anjou or Bartlett pears, peeled, halved, and cored

2 tablespoons lemon juice combined with 2 cups water

½ cup granulated sugar

1 tablespoon unsalted butter, cut into very small pieces

Batter

1¼ cups all-purpose flour

1 teaspoon baking powder

½ teaspoon baking soda

Generous ¼ teaspoon salt

Generous ¼ teaspoon ground ginger

¼ teaspoon ground cinnamon

6 tablespoons granulated sugar

1½ tablespoons unsalted butter or Browned Butter (page 147), slightly softened

1 tablespoon canola or safflower oil

1 large egg

¾ teaspooon finely grated lemon zest

2 teaspoons vanilla extract

½ cup plain nonfat yogurt

Makes 8 or 9 servings.

Preheat oven to 375° F. To prevent fruit from discoloring, stir together fruit and lemon-water in a nonreactive bowl. Turn out fruit into a colander; drain well.

Place sugar and butter in a 9-inch nonreactive metal skillet or sauté pan that can be transferred to the oven (see Note). Spread fruit over sugar, stirring to coat (pan will be very full). Place over medium heat and warm, stirring with a long-handled wooden spoon, until butter melts and fruit begins to release its juice.

French-Style Apple Upside-Down Cake

Raise heat and continue cooking, stirring occasionally, for about 15 to 20 minutes longer, until fruit is caramelized and nicely browned and gives slightly when pierced with a fork. (During the cooking, adjust heat as needed so *mixture bubbles vigorously, most of the liquid evaporates, and the thickened juices brown but do not burn.*) Remove from heat. Let cool slightly.

Arrange fruit pieces, cut sides visible, in a ring in same skillet. (If using pears, arrange with tapered ends toward center.)

To prepare batter: Thoroughly stir together flour, baking powder, baking soda, salt, ginger, and cinnamon in a medium bowl. In a mixer bowl with mixer set on medium speed, beat together sugar, butter, and oil until well blended and smooth. Beat in egg, lemon zest, and vanilla until well blended. Using a large wooden spoon, stir in yogurt. Add dry ingredients and stir just until evenly incorporated; do not overmix. Immediately spoon batter over fruit, spreading evenly to edges with a table knife.

Bake on center oven rack for 18 to 23 minutes, or until nicely browned and a toothpick inserted in center comes out clean. Let cool for 3 or 4 minutes. Center serving plate over skillet. Holding the two tightly together, invert cake onto plate. If any fruit pieces or caramel remain in skillet, spoon out and replace on cake surface. (If the fruit is not as brown as you wish, run the cake under a preheated broiler *briefly*; watch carefully and remove just as soon as the top is tinged with brown.) Let cake

stand for 5 minutes and then serve. Or let stand until cooled and then store in a cool place, covered, for up to 48 hours.

Note: Be sure to use a well-seasoned iron skillet or a nonreactive skillet, such as stainless steel, enamel-coated cast iron, or nonstick-clad (such as Teflon). Avoid unseasoned cast iron or aluminum, which can react with the acid in the fruit and lend a tinny taste. If no suitable nonreactive *and* ovenproof skillet is available, transfer the caramelized fruit and juices to a 10-inch pie plate or round casserole of similar size and depth. Top with batter and bake.

Per serving (based on 9 servings):
Calories: 227   Grams of fat: 5.9   Grams of saturated fat: 2.4
Mgrams cholesterol: 33   Mgrams sodium: 159
Percentage of calories from fat: 23

nana's orange sponge cake

*T*his is a lovely cake—light, flavorful, and more tender and moist than many sponge cakes I've tried. The recipe is one I rediscovered from my grandmother's "receipt" box. ∾ Although my grandmother's cake was always citrus-flavored, I've found that the basic recipe can be altered slightly to produce a fine almond sponge cake as well. Directions for this variation are at the end of the recipe. ∾ If you like, the cake may be drizzled with a light orange glaze.

1½ cups cake flour (unsifted)

1¼ teaspoons baking powder

¼ teaspoon salt

3 large egg yolks

1 cup granulated sugar, divided

½ cup fresh orange juice

¾ teaspoon finely grated orange zest (orange part of skin)

½ teaspoon finely grated lemon zest (yellow part of skin)

1¼ teaspoons vanilla extract

6 large egg whites, completely free of yolk

Orange Glaze (optional)

¾ cup powdered sugar

3 tablespoons fresh orange juice

2 teaspoons lemon juice

⅛ teaspoon finely grated orange zest

Makes 12 servings.

Preheat oven to 350°F. Set out a 10-inch tube pan with removable bottom. (A 9-inch tube pan *without* removable bottom may be substituted, if a ring of wax paper is inserted in pan bottom to facilitate removal of cake.)

Sift together flour, baking powder, and salt onto a sheet of wax paper. In a large mixer bowl, combine egg yolks with ¾ cup sugar and 2 teaspoons hot tap water. Beat on medium speed until foamy. Raise speed to high and continue beating for 3 to 4 minutes, or until mixture is lightened, increased in volume, and drops in slowly dissolving ribbons from beaters. In a small saucepan, heat orange juice until almost hot to the touch. To prevent splattering, lower mixer speed and gradually add juice to egg yolk mixture in a thin stream. Add citrus zests and vanilla extract. Gradually raise mixer speed to as high as possible without causing splattering and continue beating until mixture is very foamy and increased in volume, about 5 to 8 minutes longer. Working gently (so as not to deflate), gradually sprinkle flour mixture over beaten yolks and lightly fold with a rubber spatula until thoroughly incorporated but not overmixed. Set aside.

In a grease-free mixer bowl with grease-free beaters, beat egg whites on medium speed until frothy. Raise speed to high and beat until soft peaks just begin to form. Gradually add remaining sugar and continue beating until whites stand in slightly firm but not dry peaks. Using a wire whisk, mix about a third of whites into yolk mixture. Add yolk mixture back to whites and continue mixing until ingredients are evenly incorporated but not overmixed. Immediately turn out batter into pan, spreading to edges.

Bake on center oven rack for 28 to 33 minutes, or until cake is nicely browned on top and springs back when lightly pressed in center; for moistest cake do not overbake. Invert pan over neck of a bottle to keep cake suspended at least 4 inches above counter. Let stand until completely cooled, at least 1 hour.

Run a table knife around inner tube and sides of pan; for best appearance hold knife tightly against pan. Invert cake onto serving plate. Or, if desired, place cake on a wire rack set over a piece of wax paper and top with glaze.

To prepare glaze: Combine sugar, orange juice, lemon juice, and orange zest in a small saucepan. Bring to a boil over medium-high heat. Boil for 1 minute. Remove from heat and let cool for 5 minutes. Drizzle the glaze over top of cake, spreading the glaze over the top and down the sides with a table knife. Let stand for at least 15 minutes before serving.

Cake keeps, covered and at room temperature, for 2 or 3 days.

Variation: Almond Sponge Cake

Prepare exactly as for Orange Sponge Cake except omit orange zest and add 1 teaspoon almond extract along with vanilla. Omit the orange glaze from this version.

Per serving of orange or almond cake (based on 12 servings):
Calories: 139   Grams of fat: 1.4   Grams of saturated fat: 0.4
Mgrams cholesterol: 53   Mgrams sodium: 109
Percentage of calories from fat: 9

Per serving (with orange glaze):
Calories: 166   Grams of fat: 1.4   Grams of saturated fat: 0.4
Mgrams cholesterol: 53   Mgrams sodium: 109
Percentage of calories from fat: 8

fresh ginger & orange gingerbread

*F*resh ginger root and orange zest have a great affinity for one another, and in this full-bodied gingerbread they lend a distinctive, spicy-sweet aroma and vibrant, appetizing taste. Molasses enhances but does not overwhelm the other flavors. ⁓ This gingerbread can be served with either Lemon Sauce or a simple applesauce.

1⅔ cups all-purpose flour

1¼ teaspoons baking powder

½ teaspoon baking soda

1 teaspoon ground cinnamon

¼ teaspoon ground allspice

¼ teaspoon salt

1 tablespoon peeled and chopped fresh ginger root

Scant ½ cup granulated sugar

½ teaspoon finely grated orange zest (orange part of skin)

¼ cup canola or safflower oil

1 large egg white

⅓ cup light molasses

½ cup plain nonfat yogurt

1 recipe Lemon Sauce (page 137), for serving (optional)

Makes 9 servings.

Preheat oven to 325°F. Lightly grease (or spray with nonstick spray coating) an 8-inch square baking pan.

In a medium bowl, thoroughly stir together flour, baking powder, baking soda, cinnamon, allspice, and salt.

Combine ginger root, sugar, and orange zest in a food processor or blender. Process or blend until ginger is very finely ground and ingredients are blended, about 2 minutes. In a large mixer bowl, beat together oil, sugar mixture, and egg white until well blended. Beat in molasses until smoothly incorporated. With mixer on low speed, beat in dry ingredients just until smoothly incorporated. Stir in yogurt just until evenly incorporated; do not overmix.

Turn out batter into pan. Bake for 32 to 37 minutes or until center top springs back and toothpick inserted in the center comes out clean. Transfer pan to a rack and let stand until completely cooled. Cut into rectangles and serve plain or along with Lemon Sauce, if desired.

Gingerbread is best when fresh but may be stored airtight for a day or two.

Per serving (based on 9 servings):
Calories: 209   Grams of fat: 6.3   Grams of saturated fat: 0.5
Mgrams cholesterol: 0   Mgrams sodium: 169
Percentage of calories from fat: 27

Per serving (with Lemon Sauce):
Calories: 271   Grams of fat: 7.1   Grams of saturated fat: 0.8
Mgrams cholesterol: 20   Mgrams sodium: 170
Percentage of calories from fat: 23

Fresh Ginger and Orange Gingerbread with Lemon Sauce

vanilla pound cake

This is one of my favorite pound cakes, yet it is much lower in fat than most classic pound cakes. The secret to the rich taste is in browning the butter before incorporating it. This intensifies its flavor, making the most of the modest amount used. (The process of browning and rechilling the butter can be omitted if time is limited, but it is definitely worth the extra few minutes required.) ⌇ Unlike many cakes, this one is best if allowed to mellow overnight, or at least for a few hours prior to serving. It is appealing served plain but may be dressed up with the Glossy Bittersweet Glaze, if desired.

¼ cup unsalted butter

2½ tablespoons canola or safflower oil

2¼ cups cake flour (unsifted)

1¼ teaspoons baking powder

¼ teaspoon salt

1⅓ cups granulated sugar

1 large egg plus 2 large egg whites

¾ cup plain nonfat yogurt

2½ teaspoons vanilla extract

3 drops almond extract *or* ⅛ teaspoon very finely grated
    lemon zest (yellow part of skin)

1 recipe Glossy Bittersweet Glaze, page 132, for garnish
    (optional)

Makes 10 to 12 servings.

Preheat oven to 350° F. Very generously grease a 9- by 5-inch (or similar very large) loaf pan, or a 9½-inch tube pan with removable bottom. Dust pan with flour, tapping out excess.

Melt butter in a small, heavy saucepan, then bring to a boil over medium heat. Adjust heat and gently simmer for 3 to 5 minutes, until butter is just barely brown. Immediately remove from burner and transfer butter to a metal bowl or cup. Add oil. Freeze butter-oil mixture until firm but not hard, about 10 minutes. Sift together flour, baking powder, and salt onto wax paper.

In a large mixer bowl with mixer set on medium speed, beat chilled butter mixture and sugar until very light and fluffy. Add egg and whites, and continue beating until well blended and smooth. With mixer on low speed, beat in half of dry ingredients. Beat in yogurt, vanilla, almond extract (or lemon zest), and 2 tablespoons water, then remaining half of dry ingredients, just until evenly incorporated and smooth.

Turn out batter into pan, spreading to edges. Bake on middle oven rack for 50 to 60 minutes, or until a toothpick inserted in the thickest part comes out clean and the top springs back when lightly pressed. Transfer pan to wire rack and let stand until cake is *completely cooled.*

Very carefully run a knife around pan edges (and tube if tube pan is used) to loosen cake from sides and bottom. Rap pan sharply against counter several times to loosen completely. Invert and slide cake from loaf pan, or run a knife under cake bottom and then invert if tube pan is used. Transfer to a wire rack set over wax paper if adding glaze or to a serving plate if serving plain.

To garnish with glaze: Spread cool, slightly fluid glaze over top and allow excess to drip attractively down sides.

Cake can be stored, covered, for about 3 days.

Per serving (based on 12 servings):
Calories: 243   Grams of fat: 7.3   Grams of saturated fat: 2.8
Mgrams cholesterol: 28   Mgrams sodium: 105
Percentage of calories from fat: 27

Per serving (with Glossy Bittersweet Glaze):
Calories: 318   Grams of fat: 8   Grams of saturated fat: 2.8
Mgrams cholesterol: 28   Mgrams sodium: 109
Percentage of calories from fat: 22

Plum kuchen

$\mathscr{P}$lum desserts are a great favorite in Germany and Austria. This pretty plum kuchen, adapted from a recipe I collected while living in Germany, features a simple, not-too-sweet batter topped with attractively arranged slices of fresh plums. After baking, the top of the kuchen is glazed with red plum or currant jelly, which not only highlights the brilliant color of the plums but balances their tartness. Red or black plums may be used in this recipe. ∾ This kuchen is best served the day it is made, as the plums may release too much juice if allowed to stand longer. (See photograph on back cover.)

1 cup all-purpose flour

5 tablespoons granulated sugar

¾ teaspoon baking powder

¼ teaspoon salt

2 tablespoons cold unsalted butter or Browned Butter (page 147)

1 tablespoon canola or safflower oil

1 large egg white

⅓ cup plain nonfat yogurt

1 tablespoon plum brandy or kirsch (cherry brandy), or 1 tablespoon water and ⅛ teaspoon almond extract, if preferred

1 teaspoon vanilla extract

About 1⅓ pounds (about 8 medium-sized) ripe, very flavorful plums, pitted and cut into eighths

2½ tablespoons granulated sugar

¼ teaspoon ground cinnamon

½ cup red plum or red currant jelly

Makes 8 servings.

Preheat oven to 400° F. Grease (or spray with nonstick spray coating) a 10-inch springform pan.

Thoroughly stir together flour, sugar, baking powder, and salt in a medium-sized bowl. Add butter and oil to flour mixture. Using a pastry blender, forks, or your fingertips, cut in fat until mixture resembles coarse meal. In a small bowl, stir together egg white, yogurt, brandy, and vanilla, until well blended. Using a large wooden spoon, stir yogurt mixture into flour mixture until thoroughly blended but not overmixed. Spoon mixture into springform pan. Using a lightly greased table knife, spread dough to form a smooth, evenly thick layer.

Arrange plum slices, tightly fitted together in an attractive concentric circle pattern, on dough. Stir together sugar and cinnamon until mixed; then sprinkle mixture over plums.

Bake in upper third of oven for 35 to 40 minutes, or until top is bubbly and plums are cooked through when tested with a fork. Set aside on a wire rack and let cool to barely warm. Meanwhile, in a small saucepan, bring jelly to a boil. Boil 30 seconds, then immediately remove from heat and set aside until slightly thickened but still fluid. Evenly spread jelly over top of plums. Let stand until jelly is completely cooled and set. Run a small knife around kuchen and release pan sides. Serve directly from pan bottom, cut into wedges. Serve at room temperature, preferably within 12 hours of preparation.

Per serving (based on 8 servings):
Calories: 264   Grams of fat: 4.9   Grams of saturated fat: 2
Mgrams cholesterol: 8   Mgrams sodium: 114
Percentage of calories from fat: 16

harvest bundt cake with orange glaze

*T*his large, dense cake is dark, fragrant, and spicy—a little like a fruitcake, except it is made with dried and chopped fresh fruit instead of candied fruit. Though it cannot be made weeks ahead like conventional fruitcakes, it does stay moist and appealing for up to a week and freezes well.

2 cups (about 12 ounces) finely chopped pitted prunes

³⁄₄ cup orange juice

2¹⁄₃ cups all-purpose flour

1¹⁄₂ teaspoons baking powder

³⁄₄ teaspoon baking soda

³⁄₄ teaspoon ground cinnamon

¹⁄₂ teaspoon ground allspice

¹⁄₄ teaspoon salt

¹⁄₂ cup skim milk

¹⁄₄ cup canola or safflower oil

2 large egg whites

1¼ cups packed light or dark brown sugar

2 teaspoons vanilla extract

1 teaspoon grated orange zest (orange part of skin)

1½ cups (about 2 medium-sized) diced (unpeeled) tart
    cooking apples, such as Granny Smith

Glaze

⅔ cup orange marmalade (either bitter or navel orange
    marmalade may be used)

Makes 12 to 14 servings.

Preheat oven to 350° F. Generously grease (or spray with nonstick spray coating) a 12-cup Bundt pan. Lightly dust pan with flour, tapping out excess.

Combine prunes and orange juice in a medium-sized saucepan. Bring to a simmer over medium heat. Simmer, uncovered and stirring occasionally, until most of the liquid has evaporated from pan and prunes are very tender, about 10 minutes.

Meanwhile, thoroughly stir together flour, baking powder, baking soda, cinnamon, allspice, and salt in a bowl. In a large bowl, using a fork, beat together milk, oil, egg whites, brown sugar, vanilla, orange zest, and the prunes and any juice remaining in the saucepan, until very well blended. Fold apples into milk mixture until evenly incorporated. Stir flour mixture into milk mixture until thoroughly blended but not overmixed.

Spoon mixture into prepared pan, smoothing and spreading batter to edges.

Bake cake for 45 to 55 minutes or until top springs back when tapped and a toothpick inserted in thickest part comes out clean. Place pan on wire rack and let stand until almost cool, about 1 hour. Run a knife around cake edges to loosen. Invert onto wire rack and let stand until thoroughly cooled. Cake may be glazed and served or wrapped tightly and frozen, unglazed, for several weeks. Let return to room temperature before serving.

To glaze cake: Shortly before serving time, set cake on a wire rack over a sheet of wax paper. Brush any loose crumbs from cake. Bring marmalade to a boil over medium heat, then reduce heat and simmer for 30 seconds; remove from heat. Strain through a fine sieve into a bowl, then let stand until slightly thickened but not completely set. Pour glaze over cake top, smoothing evenly over surface with a pastry brush, table knife, or small spatula. Let stand until glaze sets, about 15 minutes. Using wide spatulas, transfer the glazed cake to a serving plate.

Cake may be stored, covered and refrigerated, for up to a week.

Per serving (based on 14 servings):
Calories: 295   Grams of fat: 4.3   Grams of saturated fat: 0.3
Mgrams cholesterol: 0   Mgrams sodium: 139
Percentage of calories from fat: 13

cinnamon streusel coffee cake

$\mathcal{C}$offee cakes of this type are often loaded with sour cream (not to mention butter) and are very fatty. In this one, however, the moistness and slight tang come from nonfat yogurt, which contains virtually no fat or cholesterol.

Streusel

¼ cup all-purpose flour

¼ cup packed light or dark brown sugar

2 tablespoons granulated sugar

½ teaspoon ground cinnamon

1½ tablespoons cold Browned Butter (page 147) or unsalted butter

2 teaspoons canola or safflower oil

Cake

⅔ cup coarsely chopped dark, seedless raisins

2 tablespoons rum (or substitute orange juice, if preferred)

2 cups all-purpose flour

1½ teaspoons baking powder

¾ teaspoon baking soda

¼ teaspoon salt

1¼ cups nonfat vanilla yogurt

⅓ cup granulated sugar

¼ cup packed light or dark brown sugar

1 large egg plus 2 large egg whites

½ teaspoon ground cinnamon

2 teaspoons vanilla extract

3½ tablespoons canola or safflower oil

Makes 8 to 10 servings.

Preheat oven to 350° F. Generously grease a 7- by 11-inch flat baking dish.

To prepare streusel: In a medium bowl, stir together flour, sugars, and cinnamon. Cut butter and oil into flour mixture using a pastry blender, forks, or your fingertips, until mixture is crumbly.

To prepare cake: In a small bowl, combine raisins and rum and set aside to soak for 15 minutes. In a large bowl, thoroughly stir together flour, baking powder, baking soda, and salt.

In a large bowl, using a wire whisk or a fork, whisk together yogurt, sugars, egg and whites, cinnamon, vanilla, and oil, until well blended. Using a large wooden spoon, stir yogurt mixture and raisin-rum mixture into flour mixture, just until thoroughly blended but not overmixed. Turn out batter into prepared pan. Sprinkle streusel evenly over batter.

Bake on center oven rack for 30 to 35 minutes, or until tinged with brown and a toothpick inserted in the thickest part comes out clean. Transfer to cooling rack and let stand for at least 10 minutes before serving. Coffee cake is best served warm; reheat, covered with foil, in a 325° F. oven for about 20 minutes.

Cake is best when fresh but will keep for 24 hours.

Per serving (based on 10 servings):
Calories: 299   Grams of fat: 8.4   Grams of saturated fat: 1.8
Mgrams cholesterol: 27   Mgrams sodium: 206
Percentage of calories from fat: 25

fudge bundt cake

*T*his cake is for all those skeptics who still believe dessert has to be bad for you in order to taste good. It is a dark, fudgy cake that is not only attractive but is easy to prepare also. Indeed, it is comparable to other good chocolate cakes except only 25 percent of its calories come from fat. ~ The cake is delicious plain, but I like it better drizzled with Glossy Bittersweet Glaze.

1 ounce unsweetened chocolate, coarsely broken or chopped
⅓ cup canola or safflower oil
2¼ cups all-purpose flour
½ cup plus 2 tablespoons unsweetened American-style
   cocoa powder, such as Hershey's
1½ teaspoons baking powder
¾ teaspoon baking soda
¼ teaspoon salt
1 large egg plus 2 large egg whites
2 cups granulated sugar
½ teaspoon instant coffee powder or granules
1¼ cups plain nonfat yogurt
2½ teaspoons vanilla extract
Glossy Bittersweet Glaze (page 132), optional

Makes 12 servings.

Preheat oven to 350° F. Very generously grease (or spray heavily with nonstick spray coating) a 12-cup Bundt pan.

In a small, heavy saucepan over lowest heat, combine chocolate and oil, stirring occasionally, until smooth. Set aside. Sift together flour, cocoa, baking powder, baking soda, and salt onto wax paper.

In a large mixer bowl with mixer set on medium speed, beat egg and whites, sugar, and coffee powder, until very light and fluffy. With mixer on low speed, beat in half of dry ingredients. Beat in yogurt, vanilla, ¼ cup water, the chocolate mixture, then the remaining half of dry ingredients, just until evenly incorporated and smooth.

Turn out batter into pan, spreading to edges. Bake on middle oven rack for 40 to 45 minutes or until a toothpick inserted in the thickest part comes out clean and top springs back when lightly pressed. Transfer pan to wire rack and let stand until cake is *completely cooled.*

Very carefully run a knife around pan edges and center tube to loosen cake. Rap pan sharply against counter several times to loosen completely. Holding cooling rack against pan, invert cake onto rack, transfer to a serving plate, or if glazing cake, invert onto another rack.

To glaze: Prepare the cake for glazing by brushing off any loose crumbs from its surface. Set rack and cake over a jelly-roll pan or sheet of wax paper to catch drips. Drizzle Glossy Bittersweet Glaze attractively back and forth across cake top. Let stand until glaze sets, about 30 minutes, before serving.

Cake keeps, covered, for 2 or 3 days.

Per serving (based on 12 servings):
Calories: 300   Grams of fat: 8.5   Grams of saturated fat: 0.6
Mgrams cholesterol: 18   Mgrams sodium: 171
Percentage of calories from fat: 25

Per serving (with Glossy Bittersweet Glaze):
Calories: 375   Grams of fat: 9.3   Grams of saturated fat: 0.6
Mgrams cholesterol: 18   Mgrams sodium: 179
Percentage of calories from fat: 22

fresh peach crumb cake

$\mathcal{T}$his is a wonderful way to take advantage of the enticing taste of fresh summer peaches. Moist, laden with succulent fruit, and topped with a buttery streusel, the cake tastes incredibly rich, though of course it isn't really rich at all.

Crumb Mixture

¹⁄₃ cup all-purpose flour

5 tablespoons packed light or dark brown sugar

¹⁄₄ teaspoon ground cinnamon

2 tablespoons chilled Browned Butter (page 147) or cold
    unsalted butter, cut into pieces

¹⁄₂ tablespoon canola or safflower oil

Peaches

6 tablespoons granulated sugar

2 tablespoons all-purpose flour (or up to 2 tablespoons
    more flour for very juicy peaches)

¹⁄₄ teaspoon ground cinnamon

2 pounds (10 to 12 medium-sized) fresh peaches peeled,
    pitted, and coarsely sliced

Batter

³⁄₄ cup all-purpose flour

¹⁄₂ teaspoon baking powder

¹⁄₄ teaspoon baking soda

¹⁄₄ teaspoon salt

¹⁄₃ cup granulated sugar

1¹⁄₂ tablespoons canola or safflower oil

1 large egg (or 3 tablespoons liquid egg substitute)

1¹⁄₂ teaspoons vanilla extract

Generous ¹⁄₄ teaspoon almond extract

¹⁄₄ cup plain nonfat yogurt

Makes 8 to 10 servings.

Preheat oven to 375° F. Lightly grease (or spray with nonstick spray coating) a 9-inch springform pan.

To prepare crumb topping: Combine flour, sugar, and cinnamon in food processor. Process in 6 or 7 on/off pulses until well mixed. Sprinkle butter and oil over dry ingredients. Process in on/off pulses until fat is cut in and mixture is consistency of very coarse meal. (If processor is unavailable, in a medium-sized bowl, stir together dry ingredients until mixed. Cut in butter and oil with forks or a pastry blender, until mixture resembles coarse meal.) Set aside.

To prepare peaches: In a medium-sized bowl, stir together sugar, flour, and cinnamon until well blended. Add peaches, stirring until evenly incorporated. Set aside.

To prepare batter: Stir together flour, baking powder, baking soda, and salt. In a mixer bowl with mixer set on medium speed, beat together sugar, oil, egg, vanilla, and almond extract, until well blended. Using a large wooden spoon, stir in yogurt. Add dry ingredients and stir just until evenly incorporated; do not overmix.

To assemble cake: Spread peach mixture evenly over pan bottom. Top peaches with batter, spreading evenly to pan edges using a table knife. Sprinkle crumb mixture evenly over batter.

Bake in middle third of oven for 25 to 30 minutes, until toothpick inserted in cake center comes out clean. Let cool on wire rack for 10 minutes. Run a knife around pan edge to loosen cake. Remove pan sides and transfer cake (and pan bottom) to serving plate. Cut into wedges and serve warm or at room temperature.

Cake is best when fresh but will keep, covered, for up to 24 hours.

Per serving (based on 10 servings):
Calories: 226   Grams of fat: 5.7   Grams of saturated fat: 1.8
Mgrams cholesterol: 27   Mgrams sodium: 104
Percentage of calories from fat: 22

Per serving (with egg substitute replacing egg):
Calories: 223   Grams of fat: 5.4   Grams of saturated fat: 1.7
Mgrams cholesterol: 6   Mgrams sodium: 106
Percentage of calories from fat: 21

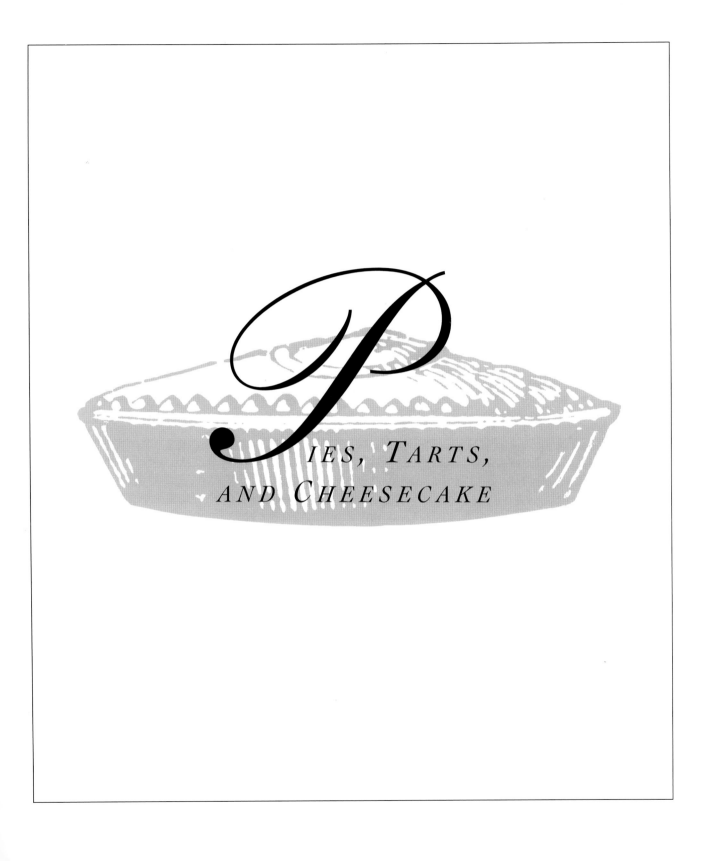

$\mathscr{P}$IES, TARTS, AND CHEESECAKE

This simple but beautiful tart celebrates the great natural appeal of oranges. A fine, translucent custard flecked with aromatic zest and colored with orange juice serves as the base. Then fresh orange slices (dabbed with apricot preserves to accentuate their color) form a gleaming mosaic over the top.

1 recipe Tart and Tartlet Pastry (pages 148–49), fitted in
   a 10-inch tart pan (preferably with removable bottom)
3½ tablespoons cornstarch
½ cup granulated sugar
1 large egg plus 1 large egg white
1 teaspoon very finely grated orange zest (orange part
   of skin)
1½ tablespoons fresh lemon juice
⅔ cup fresh orange juice
6 large, flavorful oranges, preferably navel
⅓ cup apricot preserves
Fresh red currants, for garnish (optional)

Makes 8 servings.

Preheat oven to 375°F. Prick dough all over with a fork. Cover pastry with a large sheet of heavy-duty aluminum foil, firmly smoothing foil over dough and then folding out over pan edges so pastry is completely encased.

Set tart pan on a baking sheet. Bake on center oven rack for 14 minutes. Carefully remove foil from pastry and return shell to oven. Bake for about 5 minutes longer, until tart edges are very lightly browned and center bottom is firm to the touch. Set shell and pan aside on a wire rack.

For filling: In a medium bowl, combine cornstarch, sugar, egg and white, orange zest, and lemon juice, and beat with a fork until smoothly incorporated. In a small saucepan, heat orange juice almost to a simmer. Remove from heat. In a thin stream, stir orange juice into egg mixture until evenly incorporated.

Pour mixture into partially-baked crust. Bake for 15 to 18 minutes, or until barely set when pan is jiggled. Transfer to wire rack and let stand until completely cooled.

Remove all peel and pith from oranges. Using a sharp paring knife, carefully remove each segment of the orange by cutting between the flesh and membrane on each side of it; work carefully so segments will stay intact. Lay segments on paper towels; let drain for 15 minutes. Arrange segments, spacing close together and in concentric circles, on tart filling. Cover and refrigerate tart until serving time, up to 24 hours, if desired.

Shortly before serving time, add glaze as follows: In a small saucepan, bring apricot preserves to a boil over medium heat. Simmer for 30 seconds. Remove from heat and strain through a medium-fine sieve

into a bowl. Let cool until slightly thickened but not set. Brush glaze over top of oranges. Sprinkle the currants over the surface of the tart, if using. Serve tart cut into wedges.

Per serving (based on 8 servings):
Calories: 311   Grams of fat: 7.4   Grams of saturated fat: 2.2
Mgrams cholesterol: 56   Mgrams sodium: 25
Percentage of calories from fat: 21

pumpkin pie with fresh ginger & nutmeg

Fresh ginger and nutmeg help round out and mellow the flavor of this smooth, not too spicy (but not too bland) pumpkin pie. ∼ Mixed in a food processor, the filling is quick and easy to prepare.

1 recipe Buttery Low-Cholesterol Pastry (pages 146–47),
   fitted in a 9½-inch deep-dish pie plate
¾ cup packed light or dark brown sugar
1½ tablespoons granulated sugar
¾ teaspoon ground cinnamon
½ teaspoon peeled and chopped ginger root
½ teaspoon freshly grated nutmeg (or if unavailable,
   substitute ½ teaspoon ground nutmeg)
⅛ teaspoon salt
2 cups solid pack canned pumpkin
1⅓ cups 2-percent fat milk
1 large egg plus 3 large egg whites (or substitute ¾ cup
   liquid egg substitute, if preferred)
2½ teaspoons vanilla extract

Makes 8 servings.

Preheat oven to 375°F. Prick bottom of pastry shell all over with a fork. Set aside.

In a food processor, combine brown and granulated sugars, cinnamon, ginger root, nutmeg, and salt. Process for 2 minutes. Add pumpkin, milk, egg and whites, and vanilla. Process in on/off pulses until mixed, then process continuously for 30 seconds longer. Turn out filling into pastry shell.

Bake on middle oven rack for 50 to 60 minutes, until crust is nicely browned and filling seems set in center when pie plate is jiggled. Transfer to wire rack. Let stand until completely cooled.

Serve at room temperature or lightly chilled. Store, covered and refrigerated, for 2 or 3 days.

Per serving (based on 8 servings):
Calories: 288   Grams of fat: 9.9   Grams of saturated fat: 2.5
Mgrams cholesterol: 35   Mgrams sodium: 244
Percentage of calories from fat: 31

Per serving (prepared with egg substitute):
Calories: 292   Grams of fat: 10   Grams of saturated fat: 2.5
Mgrams cholesterol: 9   Mgrams sodium: 257
Percentage of calories from fat: 31

lime chiffon angel pie

*A*lthough this pie gets only 12 percent of its calories from fat, it is still truly tempting and satisfying. To start, it is an *angel* pie (made with a meringue shell), so the crust is tasty but fat-free. And, for some inexplicable reason, when fresh lime juice, nonfat yogurt, and reduced-fat cream cheese are combined, the result is surprisingly rich.

1 baked and cooled 10-inch Meringue Pie Shell
   (pages 142–44)
⅓ cup nonfat dry milk powder, preferably a top-quality
   brand recommended for drinking
1 packet plus ½ teaspoon unflavored gelatin
¼ cup fresh orange juice
5 tablespoons fresh lime juice
1⅛ teaspoons finely grated lime zest (green part of skin)
1½ teaspoons vanilla extract
¾ cup granulated sugar
4 ounces reduced-fat cream cheese (sometimes called
   Neufchâtel cheese), softened slightly and cut into chunks
1 drop of green food color (optional)
¾ cup plain nonfat yogurt

Makes 8 servings.

Refrigerate meringue shell in pie plate while filling is prepared.

In a small bowl, gradually whisk ½ cup cold water into milk powder until completely smooth. Chill milk mixture in freezer for 45 to 50 minutes, or until frozen but not completely hard. (If you inadvertently freeze it for too long, break up with a spoon and set aside until softened *just slightly.*)

Meanwhile, sprinkle gelatin over orange juice in a small saucepan. Let stand until softened, about 5 minutes. Heat softened gelatin over medium heat, stirring until dissolved. Set aside until cooled; stir occasionally, if necessary, to prevent mixture from setting. Combine lime juice and zest, vanilla, and sugar in a blender or food processor. Blend or process until well mixed. With motor running, gradually add cream cheese chunks and food color (if used), puréeing until smooth.

Transfer frozen milk to a mixer bowl. Beat with mixer on highest speed for 5 to 7 minutes, or until mixture holds soft peaks. (Be patient, this may take some time.) Stir yogurt into cooled gelatin mixture until smoothly incorporated. Immediately add gelatin mixture to whipped milk and continue beating for 2 minutes longer. Beat in cream cheese mixture just until well blended and smooth. Spoon mixture into meringue shell.

Refrigerate for at least 30 minutes and up to 12 hours, if desired (shell gradually loses its crispness if stored longer, but the pie still tastes fine). Cut pie into wedges with a sharp serrated knife.

Per serving (based on 8 servings):
Calories: 244   Grams of fat: 3.4   Grams of saturated fat: 2.1
Mgrams cholesterol: 12   Mgrams sodium: 158
Percentage of calories from fat: 12

fresh lemon (or lime) tart

$\mathscr{S}$imple yet sophisticated, this wonderfully tangy, citrusy tart seems far more luxurious than it is. Tasters never guess—and invariably have trouble believing—that it is light on fat.

1 recipe Tart and Tartlet Pastry (pages 148–49), fitted in a
    10-inch tart pan (preferably with removable bottom)
3½ tablespoons cornstarch
¾ cup granulated sugar
1 large egg plus 1 large egg yolk
1 tablespoon grated lemon or lime zest (colored part of skin)
5 tablespoons fresh lemon juice or 4½ tablespoons fresh
    lime juice
¾ cup boiling water
2 teaspoons powdered sugar, for garnish

Makes 8 servings; variation: 8 to 12 tartlets, depending on size.

Preheat oven to 375°F. Prick dough all over with a fork. Cover pastry with a large sheet of heavy-duty aluminum foil, firmly smoothing foil over pastry and then folding out over pan edges so pastry is completely encased.

Set tart pan on a baking sheet. Bake on center oven rack for 14 minutes. Carefully remove foil from pastry and return shell and baking sheet to oven. Bake for 4 to 6 minutes longer, until tart edges are lightly browned and center bottom is firm to the touch. Set shell in pan aside on a wire rack. *Reset oven to 350°F.*

In a food processer or blender, combine cornstarch and sugar; process or blend until smoothly blended. Add egg and yolk, zest, and juice, and process or blend until smoothly incorporated. In a thin stream, add the boiling water through feed tube or hole in cap, processing or blending until it is incorporated.

Pour mixture into pre-baked crust. Bake for 18 to 23 minutes, or until just set when pan is jiggled; if necesssary, turn down heat to 325°F. to prevent crust from becoming too dark during last 5 minutes of baking. Transfer tart to wire rack and let stand until cooled. Refrigerate until chilled, at least 1 hour and up to 48 hours, if desired. Sift powdered sugar over tart top just before serving.

Variation: Lemon Tartlets

Cut out dough and fit pastry in tartlet pans as described in Tartlet Variation of pastry recipe (page 149).

Prick each shell all over with a fork. Cover each pastry with a square of aluminum foil, firmly smoothing foil over pastry and then folding out over pan edges so pastry is completely encased.

Set tartlet pans on a baking sheet. Bake on center oven rack for 8 minutes for 3-inch tartlets and 11 minutes for slightly larger ones. Carefully remove foil from pans and return to oven. Bake for 4 to 6 minutes longer, until tart edges are nicely browned and center bottoms are firm to the touch. Set pan of tartlet shells aside on a wire rack.

Ready filling as for Lemon Tart. Fill tartlet shells a scant ½ inch full. Return to oven and bake in preheated 325°F. oven for 10 to 15 minutes, until filling is just set when pan is jiggled.

44

Per serving (based on 8 servings):
Calories: 251   Grams of fat: 7.9   Grams of saturated fat: 2.4
Mgrams cholesterol: 83   Mgrams sodium: 17
Percentage of calories from fat: 28

Per serving (based on 12 tartlet servings):
Calories: 167   Grams of fat: 5.3   Grams of saturated fat: 1.6
Mgrams cholesterol: 55   Mgrams sodium: 11
Percentage of calories from fat: 28

strawberry-raspberry glaze tart

At the height of strawberry season, when succulent, unblemished strawberries are in abundance, this stunningly simple yet lush tart is not to be missed. It features plump, whole strawberries set in a brilliant red raspberry glaze upon a crisp pastry crust. The look is beautiful, the taste divine.

**1 recipe Tart and Tartlet Pastry (pages 148–49), inserted in
    a 10-inch tart pan, preferably with removable bottom**
⅓ cup plus 3½ tablespoons strawberry jelly, divided
1 tablespoon plus 1¼ teaspoons cornstarch
**1 (10-ounce) package frozen red raspberries in syrup,
    thawed**
4½ to 5 cups (about 1½ pounds) fresh strawberries

Makes 8 servings.

Preheat oven to 375° F. Prick dough all over with a fork. Cover pastry with a large sheet of heavy-duty aluminum foil, firmly smoothing foil over pastry and then folding out over pan edges so pastry is completely encased.

Set tart pan on a baking sheet. Bake on center oven rack for 15 minutes. Carefully remove foil from pastry and return shell to oven. Bake for 5 to 9 minutes longer, until tart edges are very lightly browned and center bottom is firm to the touch. Set shell and pan aside on a wire rack.

In a medium-sized saucepan, stir together 3½ tablespoons jelly, the cornstarch, and 2 teaspoons water, until blended. Place raspberries and syrup in a very fine sieve set over a bowl; force through as much pulp and syrup as possible and discard seeds. Scrape pulp clinging to underside of sieve into bowl. Stir sieved berry mixture into cornstarch mixture. Bring mixture to a simmer, stirring, over medium heat. Cook, stirring, until mixture thickens and turns clear, about 1½ minutes. Remove from heat and pour mixture evenly into pastry shell. Set aside until cooled to warm but not set, about 15 minutes.

Meanwhile, trim off cap end from strawberries so they will rest flat. Set berries, cut side down, on paper towels to blot dry for 10 minutes. Set berries, cut side down, firmly into raspberry mixture, spacing as tightly together as possible.

Bring remaining ⅓ cup strawberry jelly to a simmer over medium heat. Simmer, stirring, for 1 minute. Remove from heat and let stand until cooled and slightly thickened but not set. Using a pastry brush or table knife, spread jelly lightly over berries.

Refrigerate for at least 45 minutes and up to 24 hours before serving.

Per serving (based on 8 servings):
Calories: 273   Grams of fat: 7   Grams of saturated fat: 2
Mgrams cholesterol: 30   Mgrams sodium: 12
Percentage of calories from fat: 23

country french pear tart

*M*ild and understated, this simple French tart showcases the enticing, delicate taste of pears. It is a great contrast to the better-known, razzle-dazzle French pear desserts like Pears Helène and Pear Charlotte, which are not only more dramatic but are more complex in flavor and far richer. Indeed, it is the lack of competing elements in this dessert that allows the fine, clear pear flavor to shine.

1 recipe Citrus-Spice Tart and Tartlet Pastry (page 149), fitted in a 10-inch tart pan (preferably with removable bottom)

3 pounds (6 or 7 large) ripe Bartlett or Anjou pears

1 tablespoon fresh lemon juice combined with 1½ cups water

2 teaspoons lemon juice

½ cup granulated sugar

Generous ¼ teaspoon grated lemon zest (yellow part of skin)

Generous ¼ teaspoon peeled and finely minced fresh ginger root

3 tablespoons cornstarch

2½ tablespoons pear brandy or light rum (or substitute orange juice, if preferred)

¾ teaspoon vanilla extract

1 teaspoon unsalted butter or Browned Butter (page 147)

⅓ cup sieved apricot preserves

1 tablespoon chopped pistachios (optional)

Makes 8 to 10 servings.

Preheat oven to 375° F. Prick pastry all over with a fork. Cover pastry with a large sheet of heavy-duty aluminum foil, firmly smoothing foil over pastry and then folding foil out over pan edges so pastry is completely encased.

Set tart pan on a baking sheet. Bake on center oven rack for 14 minutes. Carefully remove foil from pastry and return shell to oven. Bake for 4 to 6 minutes longer, until tart edges are lightly browned and center bottom is firm to the touch. Set shell and pan aside on a wire rack. *Reset oven to 350°F.*

Meanwhile, peel, halve, and core pears. Cut 2 pears into even, lengthwise slices. Drop the slices into bowl of lemon-water to prevent discoloration. Coarsely chop remaining pears, tossing with 2 teaspoons lemon juice to prevent discoloration. Combine chopped pears with sugar, lemon zest, and ginger root in a large non-reactive saucepan. Bring to a simmer over medium-high heat. Adjust heat so mixture simmers gently and simmer, stirring frequently, until it cooks down to a chunky purée, 15 to 20 minutes. (Some very juicy pears will take longer to cook down.) In a small cup, stir cornstarch into brandy until smoothly incorporated. Stir mixture into saucepan and continue cooking, stirring, for about 2 minutes longer, or until mixture is thickened slightly and turns clear. Remove from heat and stir in vanilla and butter until butter melts. Spread mixture in pastry shell.

Drain pears slices. Pat dry on paper towels. Arrange pear slices attractively in concentric circles over cooked mixture. Bake for 30 to 35 minutes, until filling is bubbly and pear slices are tender when tested with a fork. Transfer tart to wire rack. Evenly brush tops of pears with apricot preserves. Let stand until cool. Refrigerate until chilled, at least 1 hour and up to 24 hours, if preferred. (Tart will still taste good but pastry may become soggy upon longer storage.) Sprinkle with pistachios, if desired.

Per serving (based on 10 servings):
Calories: 290   Grams of fat: 6.3   Grams of saturated fat: 1.9
Mgrams cholesterol: 25   Mgrams sodium: 7
Percentage of calories from fat: 19

Per serving (with pistachio garnish):
Calories: 295   Grams of fat: 6.7   Grams of saturated fat: 1.9
Mgrams cholesterol: 25   Mgrams sodium: 7
Percentage of calories from fat: 19

chocolate meringue pie

$\mathcal{B}$oasting a mellow, very chocolatey filling and billowy swirls of meringue on top, this is one of America's traditional favorites. The meringue in this version, however, is fully baked (rather than quickly run under a broiler as used to be the custom) to ensure that the egg whites are fully cooked and safe to eat. ◡ The fat in the crust and filling is pared down as much as is possible without affecting good, old-fashioned taste. The pie is still fairly rich, though, so keep portions on the moderate side. ◡ For a plain chocolate pie, the meringue can be omitted from the recipe. In this case, simply turn out filling into the baked shell, refrigerate, and serve.

1 recipe Reduced-Fat Graham Cracker Pie Shell
   (page 152), baked in a 10-inch pie plate and
   thoroughly cooled
1 recipe Chocolate Pudding (pages 81–82), freshly made

Meringue
4 egg whites, completely free of yolk and at
   room temperature
½ teaspoon cream of tartar
Pinch of salt
Generous ½ cup granulated sugar
¾ teaspoon vanilla extract

Makes 9 or 10 servings.

Preheat oven to 350° F. Turn out recipe of freshly made Chocolate Pudding into the thoroughly cooled graham cracker crust. Cover and set aside while meringue is prepared.

In a completely grease-free mixing bowl with mixer set on low speed, beat egg whites and cream of tartar until frothy. Raise mixer speed to medium and add salt. Continue beating just until very soft peaks begin forming. Immediately add granulated sugar, about a tablespoon at a time, then vanilla extract, continuing to beat on medium speed until mixture is smooth and stands in soft, fluffy peaks. Spoon dollops of mixture over surface of pie and spread out until edges are sealed and swirl with a table knife or the back of a spoon.

Place pie on rack in lower third of oven. Bake for 15 to 18 minutes, or until meringue is nicely browned all over. Transfer to wire rack and let stand until cooled to room temperature. Refrigerate, covered, for up to 24 hours. To slice pie most easily, dip knife in warm water before each cut.

Per serving (based on 10 servings):
Calories: 338   Grams of fat: 11.8   Grams of saturated fat: 5.5
Mgrams cholesterol: 47   Mgrams sodium: 202
Percentage of calories from fat: 30

Per serving (plain chocolate pie—based on 10 servings):
Calories: 294   Grams of fat: 11.8   Grams of saturated fat: 5.5
Mgrams cholesterol: 47   Mgrams sodium: 202
Percentage of calories from fat: 35

cranberry-currant pie

$\mathcal{B}$esides lending beautiful color, cranberries add a bold, sprightly fruit taste to a pie. They also blend well with other flavors. This pie, which combines cranberries with currants, apples, citrus, and spice, is reminiscent of mincemeat or raisin, but is zestier and more robust than either. ∾ The filling is on the tart side (which I think suits the cranberries), but it may be sweetened by adding a little sugar.

1 recipe Buttery Low-Cholesterol Pastry (pages 146–47), inserted in a 9½-inch deep-dish pie plate, and several pastry leaves (see Note)

1½ cups dried currants

1⅓ cups granulated sugar, or a little more if desired

3 tablespoons all-purpose flour

½ teaspoon grated lemon zest (yellow part of skin)

½ teaspoon grated orange zest (orange part of skin)

⅛ teaspoon cardamom (if unavailable, substitute cinnamon)

3⅓ cups fresh or frozen (partially thawed) cranberries, coarsely chopped

2½ cups (2 to 3 medium-sized) peeled and finely chopped tart apples, such as Granny Smith

½ teaspoon fresh lemon juice

1½ teaspoons unsalted butter or Browned Butter (page 147)

½ teaspoon vanilla extract

Makes 8 servings.

Preheat oven to 375° F. Prick pastry shell all over with a fork. Set aside.

In a small bowl, toss currants with ¼ cup hot water and set aside to soak for 10 minutes. In a large saucepan, stir together sugar, flour, citrus zests, and cardamom, until evenly blended. Stir in cranberries, apples, lemon juice, and currants and any unabsorbed water. Bring to a simmer, stirring, over medium heat. Adjust heat so mixture simmers gently and cook for about 5 minutes longer, stirring, until sugar dissolves and filling thickens slightly. Stir in butter and vanilla until evenly incorporated. Turn out filling into pastry shell, mounding slightly in center.

Bake on middle oven rack for 45 to 50 minutes, or until crust is nicely browned and filling is bubbly. Transfer to wire rack. Let stand until cooled to warm. To decorate, place the leaf shapes in the center of the pie. Serve barely warm or at room temperature.

Store, covered and in a cool place, for 2 or 3 days.

Note: If desired, when rolling out pastry, use the dough scraps to make leaves to decorate the top of the tart. After cutting out the leaf shapes, transfer them to their own baking sheet, then pull the tip of a sharp knife through the surface of each leaf to create the leaf's veining. Bake for 7 to 10 minutes, or until the edges of the leaves are tinged with brown.

Per serving (based on 8 servings):
Calories: 336   Grams of fat: 9.1   Grams of saturated fat: 2.1
Mgrams cholesterol: 7   Mgrams sodium: 154
Percentage of calories from fat: 24

deep-dish apple-crumb pie

A little cinnamon and lemon juice help heighten the flavor of this homey pie, but it is the apples themselves—preferably a blend of three different kinds—that make it memorable. I like to use a combination of Granny Smith, Winesap, and McIntosh; Granny Smith, Golden Delicious, and Jonathan are nice together, too. ∼ The tender, flaky crust and full-bodied filling make this pie seem down-right decadent.

1 recipe Buttery Low-Cholesterol Pastry (pages 146–47), rolled out and inserted in a 9½-inch deep-dish pie plate

6½ cups (about 9 medium-sized) peeled and sliced flavorful cooking apples, preferably a mixture of three kinds (see above)

1 tablespoon lemon juice

⅔ cup granulated sugar

3 tablespoons all-purpose flour

¼ teaspoon ground cinnamon

Crumb Mixture

3 tablespoons dark brown sugar

5 tablespoons all-purpose flour

⅛ teaspoon ground cinnamon

1½ tablespoons cold, unsalted butter or Browned Butter (page 147), cut into small pieces

1 teaspoon canola or safflower oil

Makes 8 servings.

Preheat oven to 400° F. Prick pastry all over with a fork. In a large bowl, toss apple slices and lemon juice.

Stir together sugar, flour, and cinnamon until well blended. Stir flour mixture into apples. Turn out into pie plate; pat down to compress mixture. (Initially, pastry will seem over-full, but apples will gradually cook down.)

For crumb mixture: Combine brown sugar, flour, and cinnamon in a food processor. Process in on/off pulses until blended. Sprinkle butter and oil over processed mixture. Process in on/off pulses just until mixture resembles coarse meal. (Alternatively, stir together sugar, flour, and cinnamon. Cut in butter and oil using your fingertips or forks.) Spread crumb mixture evenly over apples.

Bake on center oven rack for 50 to 55 minutes, or until top is bubbly and apples in center are tender when pierced with a fork. (If top or crust begins to brown too deeply, reduce heat to 375° F. during the last 10 minutes of baking.) Transfer to a cooling rack. Cool for at least 15 minutes before serving. Store, in a cool place, for up to 3 days.

Per serving (based on 8 servings):
Calories: 321   Grams of fat: 11.5   Grams of saturated fat: 3.3
Mgrams cholesterol: 12   Mgrams sodium: 155
Percentage of calories from fat: 31

summer fruit & custard tart

$\mathcal{T}$his light custard tart may be adorned with all sorts of fruit, but strawberries, blueberries, peaches, and kiwi fruit make a particularly appealing and colorful combination. ∼ You can prepare the tart with either an easy graham cracker crumb crust or with the tart pastry dough; the crumb crust is a little lower in fat. Both the shell and the custard cream can be prepared well in advance, but the tart made with graham cracker crumbs should not be assembled until shortly before serving time to keep the crust crisp. If the pastry shell is used, the tart can be assembled and then refrigerated for up to 12 hours before serving.

1 prebaked Reduced-Fat Graham Cracker Tart Shell
   (page 152) *or* 1 prebaked Tart and Tartlet Pastry shell
   (pages 148–49), baked in a 10-inch tart pan with
   removable bottom

Filling and Fruit

A *double* recipe Brandied Orange Custard Cream (page 151)

3 to 4 cups total of 3 to 5 kinds of fresh fruit, such as
   halved strawberries, halved seedless green or red grapes,
   peeled and sliced peaches or bananas (tossed with
   1 teaspoon lemon juice to prevent discoloration),
   blueberries, raspberries, pineapple pieces, and
   peeled, sliced kiwi fruit

⅓ cup apricot preserves

Makes 8 or 9 servings.

Let shell cool completely. Chill custard thoroughly. Ready fruits. Drain well and dry them between layers of paper towels.

   To assemble tart: Spread 1½ cups Brandied Orange Custard Cream in tart shell. (Reserve remaining custard for another use.) Working from edge of tart inward, arrange fruits attractively in tightly fitted or slightly overlapping concentric circles, until center is reached, embedding fruits just slightly to fix them in place. Tart may be held, refrigerated, for up to 2 hours if made with graham cracker shell, and up to 12 hours if prepared with pastry shell.

   Shortly before serving, heat apricot preserves over medium heat until fluid. Strain through a sieve into a small cup; discard pulp. Let cool until slightly thickened but not stiff. Lightly brush top of fruits with apricot preserves. Lift tart and pan bottom from sides and transfer to a serving plate. Serve immediately, cut into wedges, or refrigerate briefly before serving.

Per serving (with graham cracker crumb crust—based on 9 servings):
Calories: 254   Grams of fat: 7.1   Grams of saturated fat: 2.7
Mgrams cholesterol: 46   Mgrams sodium: 110
Percentage of calories from fat: 25

Per serving (with pastry crust—based on 9 servings):
Calories: 283   Grams of fat: 8.8   Grams of saturated fat: 3.2
Mgrams cholesterol: 69   Mgrams sodium: 27
Percentage of calories from fat: 28

deli-style lemon cheesecake

*Th*is cheesecake recipe is the result of dozens of testings and revisions and refinements spanning the course of several years. Though it is creamy and full-flavored, it has about three-fourths less fat and cholesterol than traditional cheesecakes. (A conventionally prepared cheesecake of the same size has about *35 grams of fat per serving,* while this one has about *9¼ grams per serving!* For a detailed side-by-side comparison of the two, see page 13.) ∾ The *Dream Desserts* cheesecake is good served alone, but can be topped with Blueberry Sauce (pages 130–31). Plain fresh raspberries, or strawberries tossed with little strawberry jelly also make a fine accompaniment.

Crumb Crust

Generous ¾ cup graham cracker crumbs

1 tablespoon chilled unsalted butter

½ tablespoon light corn syrup

Filling

1 cup plain, *additive-free* nonfat yogurt (see Note)

Scant 1 cup granulated sugar

Finely grated zest (yellow part of skin) of 1 large lemon

2 large eggs plus 4 large egg whites

2 teaspoons fresh lemon juice

2½ teaspoons vanilla extract

2 cups 1-percent fat, salt-free cottage cheese

12 ounces reduced-fat cream cheese (sometimes called Neufchâtel cheese), cut into chunks and at room temperature

¼ cup all-purpose flour

Makes 12 servings.

Preheat oven to 375° F. Generously grease (or spray with nonstick spray coating) the bottom of an 8½- or 9-inch springform pan. Set out a baking pan large enough to hold springform pan. To prepare springform pan for a water bath, wrap bottom in a sheet of heavy-duty aluminum foil large enough to extend up pan sides by at least 3 inches all around.

In a food processor, combine crumbs and butter. In a small cup, stir together corn syrup and ½ table-spoon water, until mixture is well blended. Add corn syrup mixture to processor. Process until mixture is well blended and begins to hold together. Add a few more drops water if mixture is too dry. Press crumbs smoothly into pan bottom. Bake for 7 to 10 minutes, until lightly tinged with brown and firm to the touch. *Reset oven to 350° F.*

Meanwhile, fold a clean, tightly-woven linen or cotton tea towel in half to yield a double layer and

place in a sieve or colander. Spoon yogurt into center of folded towel. Set aside to drain for 15 minutes. Combine sugar and lemon zest in clean food processor bowl. Process for about 1½ minutes, until lemon zest is very fine and sugar is colored yellow. Add eggs and whites, lemon juice, vanilla, and cottage cheese to sugar mixture in food processor. Process for about 2 minutes, until very smooth. Continue processing, gradually adding cream cheese chunks through feed tube, until all are incorporated and mixture is well blended. Carefully gather together edges of tea towel to form a bag around yogurt. Holding edges tightly and gently twisting, gently squeeze bag and extract *as much liquid (whey) as possible.* Spoon yogurt and flour into processor. Process just until mixture is completely smooth. Pour mixture into springform pan. Rap on counter 3 or 4 times to release air bubbles; let stand several minutes, then rap on counter again.

Place springform pan in larger pan. Set on center oven rack. Add enough hot tap water to pan to come 1 inch up springform sides. Bake on center oven rack for 30 minutes. Lower heat to 300° F. and bake for 35 minutes longer. Turn off oven; let cheesecake stand in water bath in oven for 20 minutes. Remove springform pan from water bath and transfer to wire rack; let stand until cooled. Refrigerate for at least 6 hours and up to 3 days, if desired. Top with fruit sauce or fresh berries, if desired.

Note: Check labels and be sure to choose a brand of nonfat yogurt that is free of vegetable gums, pectin, modified vegetable starch, or gelatin. Such stabilizers prevent yogurt from releasing whey, and to avoid sogginess of the crust this whey must be removed before the yogurt is used.

Per serving (based on 12 servings):
Calories: 223   Grams of fat: 9.25   Grams of saturated fat: 5.3
Mgrams cholesterol: 62   Mgrams sodium: 267
Percentage of calories from fat: 37

Per serving (with Blueberry Sauce):
Calories: 260   Grams of fat: 9.3   Grams of saturated fat: 5.3
Mgrams cholesterol: 62   Mgrams sodium: 267
Percentage of calories from fat: 32

Cookies

almond (or anise) biscotti

$\mathcal{B}$iscotti are traditional double-baked Italian cookies that are usually formed by baking logs of dough, then cutting them into slices, and baking again until crunchy-crisp. In Italy, they are often served along with coffee or wine and used as "dunkers." ∽ The following recipe can be used to prepare aromatic almond biscotti or enticing anise-flavored ones (see variation at end of recipe). Though anise is not a well-known ingredient in the United States, it is quite popular in Italy, and it lends a rich, distinctive taste to these cookies. Note that since the anise biscotti contain no nuts, they are lower in fat than the almond version.

¼ cup finely chopped slivered almonds

2¼ cups all-purpose flour

1¾ teaspoons baking powder

⅛ teaspoon salt

2 tablespoons Browned Butter (page 147) or unsalted
    butter, slightly softened

2 tablespoons almond oil or canola oil

⅔ cup granulated sugar

1 large egg plus 1 large egg white

¾ teaspoon almond extract

Makes about 30 1½- by 2¼-inch biscotti.

Preheat oven to 350° F. Grease a 12- by 15-inch or larger baking sheet; set aside.

Spread almonds in a baking dish and toast, stirring several times, for 6 to 8 minutes, until tinged with brown. Remove from oven and let stand until cooled. Thoroughly stir together flour, baking powder, and salt in a medium-sized bowl.

In a large mixer bowl, beat butter, oil, and sugar until well blended. Add egg and white, 1 tablespoon water, and the almond extract, and beat until evenly incorporated. Gradually beat in about half of flour mixture. Stir in remaining flour and almonds using a large wooden spoon. Divide dough in half. Form each half into a smooth, evenly shaped 1¼-inch-wide and 10-inch-long log by placing it on a sheet of wax paper and then rolling it back and forth until smooth. Unroll logs from paper directly onto baking sheet, spacing them at least 3 inches apart. Press down on logs to flatten slightly.

Bake logs for 26 to 29 minutes, or until lightly browned and cracked. Remove pan from oven. Slide logs onto a cutting board. Using a serrated knife and working carefully, cut logs on a diagonal into ⅜-inch-thick slices. (If they seem crumbly, let cool a few minutes before slicing.) Lay slices flat on baking sheet and return to oven. Toast for 3 to 5 minutes. Turn slices over and bake for 3 to 4 minutes longer on second side. (The longer the baking time, the crisper and drier the slices.) Transfer slices to racks and let stand until completely cooled.

Almond Biscotti and Chocolate-Hazelnut Biscotti *(recipe on pages 72–73)*

Store airtight for up to 10 days. Freeze for longer storage.

Variation: Anise Biscotti
Omit almonds and almond extract. Add 1¼ teaspoons ground anise seed (*or* generous ¾ teaspoon anise extract) *and* ½ teaspoon finely grated lemon zest when egg is added.

Almond Biscotti per serving (based on 30 servings):
Calories: 70   Grams of fat: 2.2   Grams of saturated fat: 0.7
Mgrams cholesterol: 9   Mgrams sodium: 27
Percentage of calories from fat: 29

Anise Biscotti per serving (based on 30 servings):
Calories: 64   Grams of fat: 1.8   Grams of saturated fat: 0.6
Mgrams cholesterol: 9   Mgrams sodium: 27
Percentage of calories from fat: 24

ginger crisps

$\mathcal{T}$hese fragrant, cholesterol-free crisps have an enticing (some say addictive) spice flavor, and they keep well.

2 cups all-purpose flour

2 teaspoons ground ginger

1¼ teaspoons ground cinnamon

½ teaspoon ground cloves

¼ teaspoon ground allspice

1¼ teaspoons baking powder

½ teaspoon baking soda

4½ tablespoons canola or safflower oil

⅓ cup light or dark molasses

2½ tablespoons light or dark corn syrup

⅓ cup granulated sugar

1 large egg white

1 teaspoon vanilla extract

About 2 tablespoons granulated sugar, for forming cookies

Makes about 35 2½-inch cookies.

Preheat oven to 375°F. Lightly grease (or spray with nonstick spray coating) several baking sheets.

Thoroughly stir together flour, ginger, cinnamon, cloves, allspice, baking powder, and baking soda; set aside. In a large mixer bowl with mixer set on medium speed, beat together 1 tablespoon water, the oil, molasses, corn syrup, ⅓ cup sugar, the egg white, and vanilla, until well blended and smooth. Beat in half of dry ingredients just until mixed. Using a large wooden spoon, stir in remaining dry ingredients just until evenly incorporated.

With lightly oiled hands, pull off portions of dough and shape into *scant* 1-inch balls. Space about 1½ inches apart on baking sheets. Lightly grease bottom of a flat-bottomed drinking glass. Dip greased surface into the 2 tablespoons sugar. Flatten balls to about ¼-inch thick and 1¾ inches in diameter, dipping glass into sugar after flattening each cookie to prevent glass from sticking to the next cookie. (If necessary, regrease bottom of glass once or twice.)

Bake cookies for 7 to 9 minutes or until slightly darker at the edges and almost firm on top. Remove sheets from oven and let stand for 1½ minutes. Using a spatula, transfer cookies to racks and let stand until completely cooled. Store airtight for up to 2 weeks.

Per serving (based on 35 servings):
Calories: 62   Grams of fat: 1.8   Grams of saturated fat: 0.1
Mgrams cholesterol: 0   Mgrams sodium: 27
Percentage of calories from fat: 26

oatmeal spice cookies

*T*hese large, old-fashioned cookies are made for cookie jars and lunch boxes and are great companions to a glass of milk or a cup of tea.

2 ¼ cups quick-cooking oats

2 tablespoons orange juice or water

1 cup all-purpose flour

½ teaspoon baking soda

½ teaspoon baking powder

¼ teaspoon salt

Generous ¼ teaspoon ground cinnamon

Generous ⅛ teaspoon ground nutmeg

3 tablespoons Browned Butter (page 147) or unsalted butter

3 tablespoons canola or safflower oil

1 cup packed dark brown sugar

1 large egg white

2 teaspoons vanilla extract

About 2 tablespoons granulated sugar, for shaping cookies

Makes about 35 3-inch cookies.

Preheat oven to 350° F. Generously grease several baking sheets and set aside.

Stir together oats and juice in a medium bowl; set aside. Thoroughly stir together flour, baking soda, baking powder, salt, cinnamon, and nutmeg in a medium-sized bowl; set aside. In a large mixer bowl with mixer set on medium speed, beat butter and oil until well blended and smooth. Add brown sugar, egg white, and vanilla, and beat until fluffy and smooth. Beat in the flour mixture. Using a large wooden spoon, stir in oat mixture until thoroughly incorporated.

Using lightly greased hands, press together and shape dough into 1-inch balls, spacing the balls about 3 inches apart on baking sheets. Flatten cookies into 2 ½-inch rounds using the bottom of a glass that has been lightly greased and dipped in the 2 tablespoons sugar. Dip the glass in sugar after flattening each cookie.

Bake cookies in upper third of oven for 8 to 10 minutes, or until just tinged with brown. Let stand on sheets for 3 to 4 minutes. Using a spatula, transfer cookies to racks and let stand until completely cooled.

Store airtight for up to 10 days. Freeze for longer storage.

Per serving (based on 35 servings):
Calories: 99   Grams of fat: 2.9   Grams of saturated fat: 0.9
Mgrams cholesterol: 2   Mgrams sodium: 35
Percentage of calories from fat: 26

almond tulip cups

*A*lmond tulip-shaped cookie cups make festive edible serving dishes for sorbets, ices, and fruits. They are very thin and crisp, yet fairly sturdy if handled carefully. They will wilt if exposed to humidity, however, so as soon as they cool, pack them in airtight containers. ∼ Since the cookies must be quickly lifted from baking sheets and shaped into cups while still hot and flexible, bake only one sheet at a time.

2 tablespoons unsalted butter or Browned Butter (page 147)

1½ tablespoons canola or safflower oil

¼ cup (about 2 large) egg whites

½ teaspoon finely grated lemon zest

Generous pinch of salt

¾ teaspoon vanilla extract

½ teaspoon almond extract

½ cup powdered sugar (sifted after measuring)

⅓ cup all-purpose flour

Makes 8 or 9 cookie cups

Preheat oven to 350° F. Generously grease (or spray with nonstick spray coating) several baking sheets.

Set out some custard cups or drinking glasses, bottoms facing up.

Warm butter in a saucepan over lowest heat, stirring, just until melted. Remove from heat and stir in oil. In a medium bowl, using a wire whisk, beat together egg whites, 1 teaspoon water, the lemon zest, salt, vanilla, and almond extract, until frothy. Sift powdered sugar over mixture, whisking until blended and smooth. Sift flour over mixture. Add cooled butter mixture and whisk until mixture is smooth.

Check consistency of batter by preparing a test cookie. Drop 2 teaspoons of batter on a baking sheet. Spread batter with tip of a table knife until baking sheet just shows through. Place cookie in preheated oven. If cookie does not spread at all during baking, batter is too thick; thin remaining batter with ½ teaspoon water. If batter runs and loses its shape, it is too thin; thicken the remainder by adding a teaspoon or two of flour. Bake until test cookie is rimmed with a ½-inch-wide brown edge.

For each cookie cup, drop a scant 1½ tablespoons batter, spacing portions at least 3½ inches apart on a baking sheet. (Don't crowd as cookies will spread.) Using tip of a table knife and working in a circular motion, spread batter into a 6- to 7-inch round (shape does not have to be perfect); spread *so thin that the pan surface shows through.* Sharply rap pan on counter sharply several times.

Bake rounds on center oven rack for 6 to 9 minutes, until rimmed with *1-inch of brown.* While wafers are baking, dampen some heavy-duty paper towels; they will be used to help shape cooling wafers around cups.

When wafers are ready, remove baking sheet from oven and quickly loosen wafers from sheet using a thin-edged, wide-bladed spatula. Immediately bend and shape wafers, bottom side up, around custard cup or drinking glass bottoms to form cookie cups, using dampened paper towels to hold cookies in place. (If some wafers cool and stiffen too much while others are being removed, return pan to oven for a minute or two to soften.) As soon as cups are cool enough to hold their shape, gently transfer cookies to cooling racks.

Cool, clean off, and thoroughly re-grease baking sheets before using for another pan of wafers. As soon as cookies are thoroughly cooled, pack *completely airtight.*

Store airtight, with no extra headroom in container, for up to a week. Freeze for longer storage. Handle cookie cups gently as they are fairly fragile.

Per serving (based on 9 servings):
Calories: 81   Grams of fat: 4.3   Grams of saturated fat: 1.8
Mgrams cholesterol: 7   Mgrams sodium: 42
Percentage of calories from fat: 47

iced molasses cookies

*A*ttractive, fragrant with spice, and topped with a shiny white glaze, these mild molasses cut-out cookies are good anytime, but seem particularly appropriate for the winter holidays. Since they pack and store extremely well, they make a nice gift. Strung on ribbon or yarn, they also make appealing tree ornaments. (To prepare a hole for stringing, poke a short length of spaghetti through the dough before baking. Remove the pasta lengths while the cookies are still warm.) ∾ Usually, I limit the decoration to just white or pale pastel icing, but if the cookies are to be used as ornaments or presents, a "dotted Swiss" look like that shown in the photograph makes a charming addition.

3 cups all-purpose flour

1 teaspoon baking powder

1 teaspoon baking soda

⅛ teaspoon salt

Generous 1 teaspoon ground ginger

Generous 1 teaspoon ground cinnamon

⅓ cup canola or safflower oil

1 tablespoon unsalted butter, soft but not melted

½ cup packed light or dark brown sugar

1 large egg white

Generous ½ teaspoon finely grated lemon zest
   (yellow part of skin)

¼ cup light corn syrup

¼ cup light molasses

1 teaspoon vanilla extract

Icing and Garnish

1 large egg white, at room temperature

1 teaspoon fresh lemon juice

¼ teaspoon vanilla extract

1 cup powdered sugar, sifted after measuring if lumpy,
   plus a little extra if needed

1 or 2 drops yellow or red food color (optional)

Makes 35 to 40 2½- to 2¾-inch cookies.

Preheat oven to 375° F. Generously grease several baking sheets and set aside. Thoroughly stir together flour, baking powder, baking soda, salt, ginger, and cinnamon.

In a large mixer bowl, with the mixer set on medium speed, beat the oil, butter, and brown sugar until well blended. Add the egg white, lemon zest, corn syrup, and molasses, and continue beating until thoroughly blended and smooth. Beat in the vanilla. Gradually beat in about half the dry ingredients. Using a large wooden spoon, stir in the rest of the dry ingredients until well mixed.

Divide the dough in half and wrap each portion in plastic wrap. Refrigerate for at least 1 hour (and up to 2 days, if preferred), until the dough is very cold and firm.

Working with one dough portion at a time (leave the other one refrigerated), roll out dough a scant ¼ inch thick on a lightly floured work surface. Lift dough from surface frequently and re-flour surface and rolling pin as necessary to ensure dough does not stick. Cut out cookies

using a 2½- to 2¾-inch scalloped or round cutter or drinking glass. Using a wide spatula, lift cookies and transfer to baking sheets, spacing about 1½ inches apart. Gather together scraps and rechill until firm. Roll and cut out cookies until all the dough is used. Repeat with second dough portion.

Bake cookies in upper third of oven for 6 to 9 minutes, or until edges are just barely tinged with brown; be careful not to overbake. Remove the pans from the oven and let stand for several minutes. Using a wide spatula, transfer the cookies to racks. Let stand until thoroughly cooled.

Prepare icing: With mixer set on low speed, beat egg white and lemon juice together until frothy. Add vanilla and then powdered sugar, gradually raising mixer speed and beating until icing is glossy and stiffened, about 2 minutes longer. (If, after beating, icing seems too thin, gradually beat in a few more teaspoons powdered sugar until just thick enough to spread. If it seems too thick, thin it with a few drops of water.) If preparing "dotted Swiss" decorations, set aside ¼ cup icing for forming dots; cover tightly. Add a drop or two of food color to remaining frosting to yield a pale pastel shade. Scrape down bowl sides several times. With a table knife, spread about a teaspoon of icing over each cookie to within ¼ inch of edge. Let cookies stand for about 45 minutes or until icing sets. Spoon reserved *untinted* icing into a pastry bag fitted with a fine writing tip. Pipe dots on cookies as shown in photograph. Let stand at least 1 hour, or until icing sets.

Store cookies airtight for up to 2 weeks. Freeze for longer storage.

Per serving (based on 40 servings):
Calories: 86   Grams of fat: 2.2   Grams of saturated fat: 0.3
Mgrams cholesterol: 1   Mgrams sodium: 41
Percentage of calories from fat: 23

dark fudgy brownies

*T*he secret to the mellow flavor of these moist brownies is the combination of lowfat cocoa powder with a modest helping of cocoa butter–rich unsweetened chocolate. An optional teaspoon of butter can be added to round out the flavor further.

½ teaspoon instant coffee powder or granules

⅔ cup all-purpose flour

1⅔ cups powdered sugar

¼ cup unsweetened American-style cocoa powder, such as Hershey's

¾ teaspoon baking powder

Generous pinch of salt

1½ ounces unsweetened chocolate, coarsely broken or chopped

2½ tablespoons canola or safflower oil

1 teaspoon Browned Butter (page 147) or unsalted butter (optional)

2 tablespoons light corn syrup

2 teaspoons vanilla extract

2 large egg whites

Makes 12 2- by 2⅓-inch bars.

Preheat oven to 350° F. Line an 8-inch square baking pan with aluminum foil, overlapping foil at two opposite ends by about 1½ inches. (To fit foil, invert pan and mold foil around bottom. Turn pan right side up and insert foil, folding overlapping edges outside.) Grease foil or spray with nonstick spray coating.

Stir together 1¼ teaspoons hot water and the coffee powder in a small cup. Set aside, stirring occasionally, until coffee dissolves. Sift together flour, powdered sugar, cocoa, baking powder, and salt.

In a heavy, medium-sized saucepan set over lowest heat, combine chocolate, oil, and butter (if used), stirring very frequently, until just melted and smooth; be very careful chocolate does not scorch. Remove from heat and stir in corn syrup, coffee mixture, and vanilla until well blended. Beat egg whites into chocolate mixture using a large wooden spoon. Gently stir dry ingredients into chocolate mixture just until well blended and smooth. Turn out batter into pan, spreading evenly to edges.

Bake on middle oven rack for 21 to 25 minutes, or until center top is almost firm when tapped. Transfer pan to a rack and let stand for 15 minutes. Then, using overhanging foil as handles, carefully lift brownie slab from pan and return to cooling rack. Let stand until completely cooled. Peel foil from bottom; set brownie slab right side up on a cutting board. Trim off dry edges, if necessary. Mark and then cut into 12 bars using a large sharp knife. Wipe blade with a damp cloth between cuts. Store airtight for up to 3 days.

Per serving (based on 12 servings):
Calories: 139   Grams of fat: 5   Grams of saturated fat: 0.2
Mgrams cholesterol: 0   Mgrams sodium: 55
Percentage of calories from fat: 31

Per serving (if butter is used):
Calories: 142   Grams of fat: 5.3   Grams of saturated fat: 0.4
Mgrams cholesterol: 1   Mgrams sodium: 58
Percentage of calories from fat: 33

pecan brittle cookies

*T*he wonderful crunch and nutty goodness of homemade pecan brittle plus dark brown sugar and a little butter make these unusual cookies exceptionally appealing. They are a good example of how the judicious and creative use of very fatty ingredients can yield sweets that taste rich and decadent without actually being so. ❧ For convenience, the brittle can be made up to a month ahead and refrigerated or frozen until needed.

Brittle

3 tablespoons chopped pecans

⅓ cup granulated sugar

Dough

2 cups all-purpose flour

1¼ teaspoons baking powder

½ teaspoon baking soda

Scant ¼ teaspoon salt

3 tablespoons Browned Butter (page 147) or unsalted
   butter, slightly softened

1½ tablespoons canola or safflower oil

½ cup minus 1 tablespoon light corn syrup

½ cup packed dark brown sugar

1 large egg white

2 teaspoons vanilla extract

Makes 40 to 45 2½-inch cookies.

To prepare brittle: Preheat oven to 350° F. Spread pecans in a baking dish. Place in oven and toast, stirring frequently, for 6 to 9 minutes, or until tinged with brown and fragrant; be careful not to burn. Set pecans aside to cool. Line a heatproof platter or plate with aluminum foil. Lightly oil foil.

Combine sugar and 2 tablespoons water in a small, heavy saucepan over medium-high heat. Bring to a boil, swirling mixture several times to dissolve sugar. Cook, covered, for 2 minutes. Uncover and cook, swirling pan but never stirring, for about 2 to 2½ minutes longer, or until syrup thickens slightly, bubbles, and turns deep amber but *not* dark brown. Remove pan from heat. Using a long-handled wooden spoon, immediately stir pecans into syrup, tossing to coat them; be careful not to splash as mixture is extremely hot. Immediately turn out brittle onto foil.

Let mixture stand for about 10 minutes or until cold. (Or speed up process by lifting foil and partially cooled brittle from plate and refrigerating until well chilled.) Transfer thoroughly cooled brittle to a heavy plastic bag. Crack mixture into tiny pieces using a mallet or the back of a heavy spoon. Use brittle immediately or store airtight in refrigerator or freezer for up to a month.

To prepare cookies: Preheat oven to 375° F. Lightly grease (or spray with nonstick spray coating) several baking sheets.

Thoroughly stir together flour, baking powder, baking soda, and salt; set aside. In a large mixer bowl with mixer set on medium speed, beat together butter, oil, corn syrup, sugar, egg white, and vanilla, until well blended and smooth. Beat in half of dry ingredients just until mixed. Using a large wooden spoon, stir in remaining dry ingredients and 3 tablespoons brittle mixture just until evenly incorporated. Set reserved brittle aside in a shallow bowl.

With lightly oiled hands, pull off portions of dough and press together and shape into 1-inch balls. Press top of each ball into reserved brittle until coated.

Space balls, coated side up, about 2 ½ inches apart on greased baking sheets. Moisten bottom of a flat-bottomed drinking glass by dipping in cold water; shake off excess water. Flatten balls to about ¼ inch thick and 1¾ inches in diameter with bottom of glass. (If necessary to prevent sticking, occasionally dip bottom of glass in water as you work.)

Bake on center oven rack for 7 to 10 minutes, or until cookies just begin to brown at edges; be careful not to overbake. Remove sheets from oven and let stand for 2 minutes. Using a spatula, transfer cookies to racks to cool. Cool thoroughly.

Store cookies airtight for up to a week. Freeze for longer storage.

Per serving (based on 45 servings):
Calories: 60   Grams of fat: 1.9   Grams of saturated fat: 0.6
Mgrams cholesterol: 2   Mgrams sodium: 32
Percentage of calories from fat: 28

chocolate chip-oatmeal cookies

*A*fter considerable experimentation, I've reluctantly concluded that *real* chocolate chip cookies and lowfat are contradictions in terms. This is because a cookie must seem buttery and include chocolate chips (and thus must contain a good deal of fat) in order to qualify as the real thing. ∼ The good news is I've also discovered that it is absolutely possible to create truly tempting chocolate chip cookies that contain 42 percent less fat than most ordinary chocolate chips. For example, the following chocolate chip cookies—which most definitely taste and satisfy like the real thing—have 3.5 grams of fat apiece compared to more than 6 grams for comparable "unimproved" cookies. So, while even reduced-fat chocolate chips are an indulgence, when you *must* sin, these won't send you straight to nutritional hell! ∼ Note that this recipe calls for mini-size chocolate bits. Not only do they go further, but they also make it easier to flatten the dough into cookies. If mini-chips are unavailable, substitute regular chocolate chips and chop them into smaller pieces with a large, sharp knife.

2¼ cups old-fashioned rolled oats, divided

¾ cup all-purpose flour

¾ teaspoon baking soda

¾ teaspoon baking powder

⅛ teaspoon salt

1 tablespoon plus two teaspoons skim milk

3 tablespoons Browned Butter (page 147) or unsalted butter, slightly softened

3 tablespoons canola or safflower oil

⅔ cup packed dark brown sugar

⅓ cup granulated sugar

1 large egg white

2 teaspoons vanilla extract

⅔ cup semisweet chocolate mini-chips

Makes 35 to 40 2½- to 2¾-inch cookies.

Preheat oven to 375° F. Lightly grease (or spray with nonstick spray coating) several baking sheets.

Grind 1¼ cups of the oats to a powder using a food processor or blender. (If using a blender, stop motor several times and stir to redistribute oats.) Thoroughly stir together ground oats, flour, baking soda, baking powder, and salt until well mixed. Stir together remaining 1 cup oats and milk in a small bowl; set aside.

In a mixer bowl with mixer set on medium speed, beat butter, oil, brown sugar, and granulated sugar, until light and smooth. Add egg white and vanilla and continue beating until well blended. Beating on low speed, add about half of dry ingredients until mixed. By hand, stir in remaining dry ingredients, oat-milk mixture, and chocolate bits just until evenly incorporated.

Chocolate Chip–Oatmeal and Oatmeal Spice Cookies *(recipe on page 61)*

With lightly-oiled hands, form cookies by pulling off portions of dough and pressing together and shaping into scant 1-inch balls. Space balls about 2 inches apart on baking sheets. Dip bottom of a flat-bottomed drinking glass into cold water and shake off excess. Press down each ball until about ¼ inch thick and 2 inches in diameter, dipping bottom of glass into water after flattening each cookie.

Bake in center third of oven for 6 to 9 minutes, or until cookies are just barely tinged with brown at edges. (They will be soft and seem underdone but will firm up when cool; do not overbake). Let baking sheets stand to cool for 2 minutes. Using a spatula, transfer cookies to wire racks. Let stand until completely cooled.

Store cookies airtight for up to a week. (For longer storage, freeze in an airtight container.)

Per serving (based on 40 servings):
Calories: 92   Grams of fat: 3.5   Grams of saturated fat: 0.7
Mgrams cholesterol: 2   Mgrams sodium: 31
Percentage of calories from fat: 34

chocolate-hazelnut (or double chocolate) biscotti

*T*talian dessert makers often pair chocolate and hazelnuts, a combination I find extraordinarily good. Though nuts are quite oily and must be used sparingly in reduced-fat recipes, hazelnuts are so flavorful that even a small quantity can contribute a great deal to the appeal of a dessert. In the case of these crunchy-crisp biscotti, the nutty flavor is intensified even further by using hazelnut oil in place of some of the butter that would normally be called for. ➴ For those who cannot obtain hazelnuts or do not care for them (the latter possibility is difficult for me to imagine!), I have provided a double chocolate biscotti recipe in which chocolate chips are substituted for the nuts (see variation at end of recipe). The nutless version is not classic Italian, but it is still good, not to mention slightly lower in fat.

¼ **cup hazelnuts**

2 ⅓ **cups all-purpose flour**

1 ¾ **teaspoons baking powder**

¼ **teaspoon salt**

2 ½ **tablespoons hazelnut oil (if unavailable, substitute canola oil)**

2 tablespoons unsalted butter or Browned Butter
   (page 147), slightly softened

1 cup granulated sugar

4½ tablespoons unsweetened American-style cocoa powder,
   such as Hershey's

½ teaspoon instant coffee powder or granules

3 large egg whites

1½ teaspoons vanilla extract

A few drops almond extract

Makes about 35 1¼- by 3-inch biscotti.

Preheat oven to 350°F. Grease a large baking sheet
and set aside.

Spread hazelnuts in a baking pan and toast, stirring
occasionally, for 16 to 19 minutes, or until hulls loosen
and nuts are nicely browned. Set aside until cooled.
Remove and discard any loose hulls from nuts by rubbing them between your hands or in a clean kitchen
towel. Chop nuts fairly fine. Thoroughly stir together
nuts, flour, baking powder, and salt.

In a large mixer bowl, beat oil, butter, sugar, cocoa,
and coffee powder until well blended. Add egg whites,
vanilla, almond extract, and 2½ tablespoons water,
and beat until evenly incorporated. Gradually beat in
half of flour mixture. Stir in remaining flour mixture
using a large wooden spoon. Cover and refrigerate for
10 minutes. Divide dough in half. Form each half into
a log. Lengthen each into a smooth, evenly shaped
1¼-inch-wide and 11-inch-long log by rolling it back
and forth on a sheet of wax paper. Roll logs onto
baking sheet, spacing at least 3 inches apart.

Bake logs for 27 to 29 minutes or until cracked and
almost firm when pressed in center top. Remove pan
from oven. Slide logs onto a cooling rack. Let stand
until completely cooled, about 45 minutes.

Preheat oven to 350°F. Transfer cooled logs to
cutting board. Using an electric knife or large, sharp
knife, cut logs on a diagonal into ⅜-inch-thick slices.
(Work carefully as logs may be slightly crumbly.)
Return slices to baking sheet, laying them flat.
Bake for 8 to 10 minutes more (the longer the baking
time, the crunchier the biscotti). Let stand until
completely cooled.

Store airtight for up to 2 weeks. Freeze for longer
storage.

Variation: Double Chocolate Biscotti

Substitute ¼ cup coarsely chopped semisweet chocolate chips for ¼ cup hazelnuts. Combine chocolate
chips with dry ingredients in place of hazelnuts and
proceed as directed.

Per serving Chocolate-Hazelnut Biscotti (based on 35 servings):
Calories: 72   Grams of fat: 2.4   Grams of saturated fat: 0.5
Mgrams cholesterol: 2   Mgrams sodium: 37
Percentage of calories from fat: 29

Per serving Double Chocolate Biscotti (based on 35 servings):
Calories: 74   Grams of fat: 2.2   Grams of saturated fat: 0.5
Mgrams cholesterol: 2   Mgrams sodium: 38
Percentage of calories from fat: 26

chocolate-hazelnut meringue kisses

*T*hese delicious, melt-in-your-mouth kisses contain less than 1 gram of fat apiece compared to 6 to 8 grams for regular flour-based chocolate-nut cookies. ❧ The kisses are most attractive if formed using a pastry bag, but may also be simply shaped with spoons.

¼ cup hazelnuts

½ ounce unsweetened chocolate, grated

¼ cup unsweetened American-style cocoa powder,
   such as Hershey's

3 tablespoons cornstarch

½ cup powdered sugar (sifted after measuring)

½ teaspoon instant coffee powder or granules

¾ teaspoon vanilla extract

⅛ teaspoon almond extract

3 large egg whites, at room temperature and completely
   free of yolk

⅛ teaspoon salt

⅔ cup granulated sugar

Makes 30 to 35 2¼-inch cookies.

Preheat oven to 350° F. Line several large baking sheets with baking parchment. (Wax paper sprayed with nonstick spray coating may be substituted, but may smoke slightly.)

Spread hazelnuts in a baking pan and toast, stirring occasionally, for 15 to 17 minutes or until hulls loosen and nuts are browned. Set nuts aside until cool. *Reset oven to 275° F.*

Remove and discard loose bits of hull from cooled hazelnuts by rubbing them between your hands or in a clean kitchen towel. Chop nuts fairly fine. In a bowl, stir together nuts, chocolate, cocoa powder, cornstarch, and powdered sugar, until well blended. In a cup, stir together coffee powder, ½ teaspoon hot water, vanilla, and almond extract, until coffee dissolves. Set aside.

In a completely grease-free mixing bowl with mixer set on medium speed, beat egg whites until very frothy. Raise mixer speed to high and add salt. Beat *just until very soft peaks begin forming.* Immediately begin adding granulated sugar, 2 tablespoons at a time, continuing to beat until all the sugar is incorporated and mixture is stiff, smooth, and glossy, about 3 minutes. Beat coffee mixture into meringue until smoothly incorporated. Using a rubber spatula, fold in cocoa-nut mixture until evenly incorporated but not overmixed. Spoon mixture into a pastry bag fitted with a ½-inch diameter plain tip. Pipe into 1¼-inch diameter kisses, spacing about 1½ inches apart. (Alternatively, drop mixture by small rounded teaspoonfuls about 1½ inches apart.)

Bake cookies on center oven rack for 17 to 20 minutes, or until firm on the outside and slightly soft inside. Remove from oven and let stand, still attached to paper, until completely cooled. Carefully peel kisses from paper.

Store airtight for 3 or 4 days. Freeze for longer storage.

Per serving (based on 35 servings):
Calories: 32   Grams of fat: 0.8   Grams of saturated fat: 0
Mgrams cholesterol: 0   Mgrams sodium: 12
Percentage of calories from fat: 22

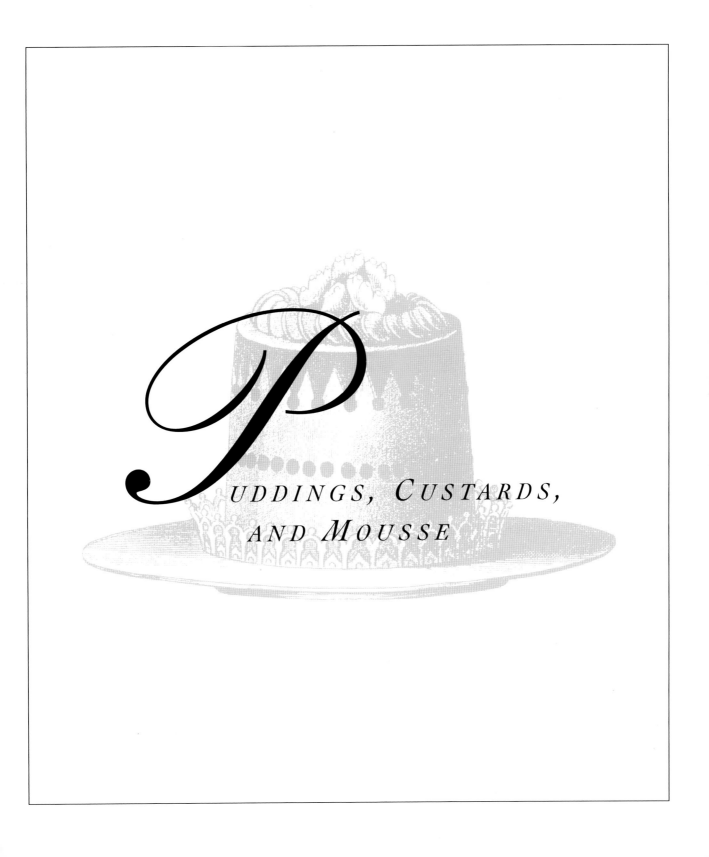

*P*UDDINGS, CUSTARDS, AND MOUSSE

raspberry-plum summer pudding

*T*he combination of raspberries and plums makes an exceptionally flavorful summer pudding. Despite its name, the dessert needn't be served only in summer. Plums are available in great variety and abundance from late spring through early fall, and frozen raspberries are stocked in supermarkets year-round. If you can obtain some fresh black raspberries, add one-half cup of these along with the red raspberries to heighten the pudding's flavor even more. ～ This dessert is extremely low in fat, but nevertheless tastes quite satisfying.

1 (10-ounce) package frozen red raspberries in syrup,
    partially thawed

1 tablespoon fresh lemon juice

Finely grated zest (yellow part of skin) of 1 large lemon

1 packet plus 1¼ teaspoons unflavored gelatin

2 pounds (about 12 medium) ripe black plums, pitted
    and chopped

2 tablespoons kirsch (cherry brandy) or orange juice,
    if preferred

⅔ cup granulated sugar

⅛ teaspoon ground cinnamon

8 to 10 slices thinly sliced (compact, not fluffy) home-style
    white or oatmeal bread (such as Pepperidge Farm),
    crusts removed

Fresh plum slices and red or black raspberries, for garnish
    (optional)

Mint sprigs, for garnish (optional)

Dollops (3 tablespoons) of Fruit Crème (page 140), for
    garnish (optional)

Makes 6 to 7 servings.

Line a 1½-quart (or slightly larger) soufflé dish, charlotte mold, or round mold with plastic wrap,

carefully smoothing wrap into bottom and sides and allowing plastic to overhang by 1 inch all the way around. Drain syrup from raspberries into a cup. Add lemon juice and zest to syrup. Sprinkle gelatin over syrup; set aside to soften for 5 minutes.

Combine plums, kirsch, sugar, and cinnamon in a medium-sized saucepan. Bring to a simmer over medium heat, stirring until sugar dissolves. Gently simmer for 8 to 11 minutes or until plums are just tender. Stir in gelatin mixture and simmer, stirring until gelatin dissolves, about 1 minute longer. Remove pan from heat. Gently stir in raspberries and any remaining syrup.

Arrange slices of bread in bottom of dish, cutting as needed and fitting together tightly. Arrange more slices all around dish sides, fitting them together tightly and forming an even edge. Spoon fruit mixture into center of dish, taking care not to dislodge strips and jiggling dish to even surface. If bread around sides extends more than ⅛ inch above fruit, trim to ⅛ inch, using a paring knife. Cover surface with plastic wrap. Refrigerate for at least 4 hours, or until set, and up to 48 hours.

To serve: Invert dish over serving plate, using overhanging plastic wrap as handles to loosen pudding from dish. Center pudding on plate. Peel off plastic wrap. Garnish top of pudding with plum slices and raspberries, if desired. Arrange mint sprigs around pudding sides and top, if desired. Cut into wedges and serve. Garnish individual servings with Fruit Crème, if desired.

Per serving (based on 7 servings):
Calories: 272   Grams of fat: 1.2   Grams of saturated fat: 0
Mgrams cholesterol: 0   Mgrams sodium: 82
Percentage of calories from fat: 4

Per serving (with Fruit Crème garnish):
Calories: 340   Grams of fat: 3.2   Grams of saturated fat: 1.2
Mgrams cholesterol: 7   Mgrams sodium: 117
Percentage of calories from fat: 8

chocolate soufflé

*C*hocolate soufflé has the reputation of being difficult to make, probably because it puffs up so impressively during baking and falls so rapidly when it cools. In fact, it is nothing more than an airy, chocolatey baked pudding that is fluffed up high with beaten egg whites. The only real challenge in preparing it is making sure that you are ready when the soufflé is—once removed from the oven, it waits for no one. ❧ The soufflé may be served alone or dressed up with Brandied Orange Custard Sauce.

⅓ cup skim milk

3½ tablespoons cornstarch

2 tablespoons unsweetened cocoa powder

½ teaspoon instant coffee powder or granules

2 tablespoons orange juice

½ tablespoon unsalted butter, cut into pats

1½ ounces unsweetened chocolate, chopped moderately fine

1½ teaspoons vanilla extract

1 tablespoon cognac or good-quality brandy

1 tablespoon Grand Marnier

2 large egg yolks

Pinch of salt

¾ cup plus 2 tablespoons granulated sugar, divided

7 large egg whites, completely free of yolk and at room temperature

¼ teaspoon cream of tartar

About 1 tablespoon powdered sugar, for garnishing soufflé top

1 recipe Brandied Orange Custard Sauce (page 151), optional

Makes 5 or 6 servings.

Adjust rack to lower third of oven and preheat oven to 400° F. Generously grease (or spray with nonstick coating) a 1½-quart soufflé dish (see Note). Fit soufflé dish with a 4-inch-wide aluminum foil collar. (To prepare collar, tear off a sheet of foil long enough to fit around rim of soufflé dish and slightly overlap itself. Fold foil over several times to form a band at least 4 inches wide. With band extending at least 2 inches above rim, wrap band around outside edge of dish, overlapping ends and fastening securely with straight pins or string.)

Combine milk and cornstarch in a medium-sized, heavy saucepan, whisking until well blended. Vigorously whisk in cocoa powder and coffee, then orange juice, until smoothly incorporated. Add butter. Heat mixture over medium heat, stirring vigorously, until butter melts and mixture comes to a simmer. Cook, stirring, until mixture thickens, about 1 minute. Remove from heat. Add chocolate to mixture, stirring until completely melted and smooth. Stirring vigorously, add vanilla, cognac, and Grand Marnier. Set aside.

In a mixer bowl, beat egg yolks, salt, and half of sugar, until blended. Continue beating on high speed for 4 to 5 minutes. until mixture is lightened and thick and drops from beaters in slowly flowing ribbons. Adding a small amount at a time, stir egg mixture into chocolate mixture until well blended and smooth.

In a large, completely grease-free mixer bowl with mixer set on medium speed, beat whites and cream of tartar until very frothy. Raise speed to high and beat until whites just begin to form peaks. Gradually add remaining sugar, continuing to beat until stiff but not dry peaks form. Using a wire whisk, whisk about a cup of whites into chocolate mixture. Add chocolate mixture back to remaining egg whites, whisking until completely blended but not overmixed. Spoon mixture into prepared soufflé dish.

Set soufflé dish on a baking sheet. Bake for 20 minutes. Lower oven temperature to 375° F. and continue baking for 14 to 18 minutes, or until center top is puffy (center will still be moist and look underdone). Sift a light dusting of powdered sugar over top of soufflé. Serve immediately, along with Brandied Orange Custard Sauce, if desired.

Note: Differing methods of sizing soufflé dishes among foreign and domestic manufactuers can lead to confusion. Choose a dish that *holds* 1½ quarts when filled.

Per serving (based on 6 servings):
Calories: 238   Grams of fat: 6.8   Grams of saturated fat: 1.2
Mgrams cholesterol: 74   Mgrams sodium: 120
Percentage of calories from fat: 24

Per serving (with Brandied Orange Custard Sauce):
Calories: 330   Grams of fat: 9.5   Grams of saturated fat: 2.6
Mgrams cholesterol: 117   Mgrams sodium: 137
Percentage of calories from fat: 25

caramel-glazed ginger custards

*T*his is my slimmed-down version of Crème Caramel, the classic caramel-glazed custard dessert. Mild and smooth and scented with ginger and orange, the little unmolded custards are good served alone, but are also delicious with a fruit garnish, such as the Autumn Fruit Compote. (Or for an even simpler garnish, sprinkle a few raspberries around each custard.) ~ If planning to serve the custards with the compote, use eight very small cups; if serving alone, use six slightly larger ones.

Caramel
½ cup granulated sugar

Custard
2½ cups 2-percent fat milk
1 (3-inch) piece vanilla bean (see Note)
⅓ cup granulated sugar
1 teaspoon peeled and chopped fresh ginger root
Pinch of grated orange zest
Pinch of salt
2 large eggs plus 2 large egg whites
½ recipe Autumn Fruit Compote (page 101), for garnish
  (optional)

Makes 6 servings (or 8 servings with compote).

Preheat oven to 350° F. Set 6 to 8 custard cups or heat-proof ramekins in a pan large enough to hold them. Warm the cups by adding ½ inch very hot water to pan.

To prepare caramel: In a small saucepan over medium-high heat, bring sugar and 3 tablespoons water to a simmer. Cover and boil for 1 minute to allow steam to wash sugar from pan sides. Uncover and continue boiling, lifting pan and gently swirling occasionally (but never stirring), until sugar turns a medium caramel color. Immediately lift pan from heat. Working carefully (mixture is extremely hot) and dividing caramel syrup among the cups, pour syrup into each one, immediately tipping cup from side to side to coat as much of its surface as possible. Set coated cups aside to allow caramel to cool and firm. (If caramel stiffens as you work, reheat it until fluid and then continue.)

To prepare custard: In a medium saucepan over medium-high heat, bring milk and vanilla bean just to a simmer. Remove from heat and set aside to cool to barely hot. Combine sugar, ginger root, orange zest, and salt in a food processor. Process for about 1 minute, until mixture is smooth. Add eggs and whites and process in on/off pulses just until mixed. Remove vanilla bean from milk. Processing in on/off pulses, add about a third of milk through feed tube; then slowly stir processed mixture back into remaining milk. Strain mixture through a fine sieve and divide among prepared cups. Return cups to larger pan and transfer to lower rack of oven.

Add enough hot water to pan to reach halfway up sides of cups. Bake for 25 to 30 minutes, or just until custards appear set when cups are jiggled. Remove cups to wire racks and let stand to cool. Refrigerate until chilled, at least 45 minutes (and up to 3 days), before serving. Run a knife around custards to loosen, then invert onto serving plates. Serve plain, or garnish each custard with about ¼ cup Autumn Fruit Compote.

Note: If vanilla bean is unavailable, substitute 2 teaspoons vanilla extract. Add when eggs and whites are added.

Per serving (based on 6 servings):
Calories: 165   Grams of fat: 3.5   Grams of saturated fat: 1.6
Mgrams cholesterol: 77   Mgrams sodium: 130
Percentage of calories from fat: 18

Per serving (based on 8 servings with compote garnish):
Calories: 241   Grams of fat: 2.6   Grams of saturated fat: 1.2
Mgrams cholesterol: 58   Mgrams sodium: 101
Percentage of calories from fat: 11

chocolate pudding (or filling)

*D*oubtless, legions of American children think that chocolate pudding is the brown, vaguely cocoa-like mixture that comes from a box. The misconception really needs to be corrected, and this delicious, very quick chocolate pudding will do the job. It is almost as fast and easy to whip up as the packaged version, but the taste—a deep, rich chocolate—is in a whole different league. The secret is in generous quantities of fine-quality chocolate; I especially like to use Lindt Excellence or Callebaut bittersweet in this pudding. ∼ Due to the cocoa butter contributed by the chocolate, this recipe is a bit of an indulgence. However, since it contains only skim milk and no cream or butter, it has about 20 percent less fat than comparable puddings, while actually delivering much greater chocolate satisfaction per bite. ∼ This recipe serves as a chocolate filling in the Chocolate Meringue Pie, page 49.

¼ cup cornstarch

3 tablespoons all-purpose flour

2½ tablespoons unsweetened cocoa powder

¾ teaspoon instant coffee powder or granules

¾ cup packed light brown sugar

⅛ teaspoon salt

2 large egg yolks

3 cups skim milk

4½ ounces chopped fine-quality bittersweet
    (not unsweetened) or semisweet chocolate

1 tablespoon cognac or good quality brandy, optional

2½ teaspoons vanilla extract

Makes 6 servings.

In a large, heavy saucepan, stir together cornstarch, flour, cocoa powder, coffee powder, brown sugar, and salt, until well blended. Whisk in egg yolks and about ¾ cup milk, stirring vigorously until smoothly incorporated. Stir in remaining milk. Bring mixture to a boil over medium heat, whisking vigorously. Boil for *2 full minutes*, stirring constantly and scraping pan bottom to prevent scorching; do not undercook. Remove from heat. Stir in chocolate until completely melted and smooth. Stir in cognac (if used) and vanilla. Turn out into individual pudding dishes or a large bowl and cover tightly with plastic wrap. (Alternatively, if using in place of a pastry cream filling, turn out into a storage container. Lay a sheet of wax paper against surface to prevent skin from forming.) Refrigerate for at least 1½ hours and up to 48 hours before serving.

Per serving (based on 6 servings):
Calories: 249   Grams of fat: 10.1   Grams of saturated fat: 5.5
Mgrams cholesterol: 55   Mgrams sodium: 90
Percentage of calories from fat: 34

molded rum cream puddings with two sauces & fruit

𝒯his dessert sets the silky smoothness and mild, mellow flavor of individual rum-laced puddings against the brilliant colors and zestiness of apricot and raspberry sauces and a few bits of fruit. It is striking-looking yet easy-to-create. ∾ For convenience, the puddings, sauces, and fruit can all be readied well ahead. (See photograph on front cover.)

1 envelope unflavored gelatin

3 tablespoons light or dark rum

1½ tablespoons cornstarch

6½ tablespoons granulated sugar

Pinch of very finely grated lemon zest (yellow part of skin)

1 large egg yolk

1⅔ cups skim milk, divided

2¼ teaspoons vanilla extract

4 drops almond extract

Scant ¼ cup heavy (whipping) cream

Garnish

1 recipe Apricot Sauce (page 131)

1 recipe Quick Raspberry Sauce (page 135)

1 cup assorted fresh berries and/or fruit, such as raspberries, strawberry halves, sliced plums, peeled and sliced kiwi fruits, blackberries, blueberries, or orange segments

Makes 5 or 6 servings.

Lightly oil 5 or 6 ½- to ⅔-cup decorative molds, custard cups, or small ramekins.

In a small cup, sprinkle gelatin over rum. Set aside until gelatin softens, about 5 minutes. In a medium saucepan, stir together cornstarch, sugar, and lemon zest, until well blended. Whisk in gelatin mixture until smoothly incorporated. Whisk in egg yolk, stirring well. Stir in 1 cup milk. Bring mixture to a *full boil* over medium heat, stirring. Boil for 1½ minutes, stirring constantly; remove from heat. Immediately stir remaining milk, vanilla, and almond extract into egg mixture. Remove from heat, stirring, and strain through a sieve into a bowl. Set aside.

In a mixer bowl with mixer set on high speed, whip cream to soft peaks. Set custard mixture in a bowl of ice. Whisk, scraping sides of bowl frequently, until mixture thickens and just begins to jell. Whisk cream into custard mixture until smoothly blended. Turn out mixture into individual molds, dividing equally among them.

Refrigerate molds for at least 1½ hours and up to 48 hours before serving. To unmold, dip each mold in hot water for 5 seconds. Insert tip of a table knife to loosen each pudding and invert onto serving plate. Garnish plates by spooning generous pools of apricot sauce and smaller pools of raspberry sauce decoratively around each pudding. Add a few berries or bits of fruit to each plate and serve.

Per serving (based on 6 servings):
Calories: 300   Grams of fat: 4.7   Grams of saturated fat: 2.4
Mgrams cholesterol: 49   Mgrams sodium: 44
Percentage of calories from fat: 14

lemon souffléed pudding

*T*his is a puffy, fragrant, very lemony dessert, a sort of soufflé, custard, and sauce all rolled into one. Souffléed puddings, or puff puddings as they are also called, are good, old-fashioned American desserts. Usually, they are served warm, but this one is also nice chilled.

1 cup granulated sugar, divided

¼ cup cornstarch

3 tablespoons all-purpose flour

3 large egg yolks

1¾ cups 2-percent fat milk, divided

1 tablespoon Browned Butter (page 147) or unsalted butter, slightly softened

⅛ teaspoon salt

6½ tablespoons fresh lemon juice

Generous 2¾ teaspoons finely grated lemon zest (yellow part of skin)

1½ teaspoons vanilla extract

5 large egg whites, completely free of yolk

Makes 6 or 7 servings.

Preheat oven to 350° F. Generously grease a 2½-quart casserole or soufflé dish. Set out a baking pan large enough to hold the casserole.

In a medium-sized saucepan, stir together ¾ cup sugar, cornstarch, and flour until well mixed. Gradually stir in egg yolks and 1 cup milk until smoothly incorporated. Bring mixture to a boil, stirring, over medium-high heat. Boil, stirring or whisking vigorously, for 1 minute. Remove from heat and stir in butter, salt, and lemon juice and zest, until smoothly incorporated. Stir in remaining milk, then vanilla, and set aside.

In a separate, completely grease-free mixer bowl with mixer set on medium speed, beat egg whites until frothy and opaque. Raise speed to high and continue beating until soft peaks just begin to form. Gradually beat in remaining granulated sugar, continuing to beat until mixture stands in firm but not dry peaks. Add

1 cup egg white mixture to custard mixture, folding with a wire whisk until evenly incorporated. Then, fold custard mixture back into whites until smoothly incorporated but not overmixed. Turn out mixture into soufflé dish. Immediately place dish in larger pan and transfer to center oven rack. Add enough hot tap water to come 1 inch up casserole sides.

Bake for 25 to 35 minutes, or until mixture is almost firm when pan is jiggled and top is tinged with brown. Remove large pan from oven; let soufflé dish stand in water bath for 10 to 15 minutes. Serve souffléed pudding warm, spooned into bowls. Alternatively, cover and refrigerate for up to 3 days; rewarm in a 250° F. oven or serve chilled.

Per serving (based on 7 servings):
Calories: 222   Grams of fat: 5.1   Grams of saturated fat: 2.5
Mgrams cholesterol: 101   Mgrams sodium: 112
Percentage of calories from fat: 20

charlotte royale

*T*he classic French dessert called Charlotte Royale takes its name from the royal-red (raspberry-filled) cake pinwheels that stud its entire surface and surround a smooth, creamy mousse. Here, the look and taste are as impressive as ever, but the fat content is lower (about 4 grams per serving, compared to 20 to 30 or more for traditional versions). ∾ Since this can be made ahead, looks sumptuous, and is easy to serve, it makes a fine finale for a dinner party.

1 (10-ounce) package frozen red raspberries in syrup, thawed

¼ cup red raspberry jelly or sieved red raspberry preserves

2 teaspoons kirsch (cherry brandy), or substitute orange juice, if preferred

1 teaspoon cornstarch

Charlotte Royale

1 Lemon Roulade (pages 144–45), rolled up from a longer
  side to yield a 15-inch-long log, thoroughly cooled
1 recipe Lemon Chiffon Mousse (pages 88–89)
⅔ to ¾ cup sieved apricot preserves
½ cup fresh red raspberries, for garnish (optional)

Makes 8 to 10 servings.

Prepare cake pinwheels: Press raspberries and syrup through a fine sieve into a medium-sized saucepan. Scrape any pulp clinging to underside of sieve into saucepan. Stir in raspberry jelly and bring to a simmer over medium heat. Simmer for 7 minutes, stirring occasionally to prevent sticking or burning. In a small cup, stir together kirsch and cornstarch until well blended. Whisk into saucepan and continue to simmer until mixture thickens slightly and clears. Remove from heat and set aside until mixture cools and thickens but is still slightly fluid and spreadable. Unroll thoroughly cooled cake roll. Cover cake surface evenly with raspberry mixture, brushing with pastry brush or spreading with long-bladed spatula. (Either reserve any remaining raspberry mixture for another use or discard.) Working from a long side, roll up cake neatly and tightly. Wrap tightly in a clean sheet of wax paper, folding or twisting ends to keep paper from unwrapping. Transfer roll to tray and place in freezer until roll is very well chilled, at least 3 hours and preferably 8 hours.

Line interior of a 2½-quart or similar kitchen bowl with tapered bottom with plastic wrap, smoothing wrap as much as possible and leaving several inches of wrap overhanging rim on all sides. Slice chilled cake roll crosswise into 3/16-inch slices using a large serrated knife and a sawing motion. Arrange slices tightly together in a circular pattern in bottom of

bowl. Then add two rows around bowl sides, spacing as close together as possible. Press down on slices to fill any gaps. Cut any remaining pinwheel slices in half. If there are enough to form a third row around both sides, fit them into place; otherwise reserve them. Cover bowl with wax paper and set aside.

Prepare Lemon Chiffon Mousse as directed. Spoon mousse into pinwheel-lined bowl, working carefully so as not to dislodge the slices. If there were not enough leftover pinwheel half-slices to form a third ring, lay remaining half-slices flat on mousse around perimeter of bowl, spacing them evenly. Rap bowl on counter several times to eliminate air pockets. Cover bowl with plastic wrap and press down to compact mixture slightly. Refrigerate for at least 3 hours, until mousse is thoroughly chilled, and up to 24 hours, if desired. (Charlotte may also be frozen, tightly wrapped, for up to a week. Thaw completely in refrigerator before serving.)

To garnish and serve charlotte: In a small saucepan over medium-high heat, heat apricot preserves until boiling. Lower heat and simmer 30 seconds longer. Set aside until cooled and slightly thickened but still fluid. Loosen and lift dessert from bowl, using overlapping plastic wrap as handles. Center charlotte on serving plate and lift off plastic wrap. Lightly brush surface of charlotte with apricot preserves until glazed all over. If necessary, wipe rim of plate clean with damp paper towels. Return to refrigerator until glaze cools and sets. If desired, just before serving, garnish edge of charlotte with fresh raspberries. Cut into wedges using a large, sharp knife and transfer to individual serving plates.

Per serving (based on 10 servings):
Calories: 295   Grams of fat: 4.1   Grams of saturated fat: 2.2
Mgrams cholesterol: 53   Mgrams sodium: 124
Percentage of calories from fat: 12

strawberry-peach bavarian cream with melba sauce

*T*he combination of fresh, sweet strawberries and peak-of-season peaches is absolutely glorious in this airy but sumptuous Bavarian cream. The dessert is also rather elegant, particularly if made in a ring or other shape that can be filled with whole strawberries and peach slices and presented on a pool of melba sauce. ⌒ This makes a memorable summer dessert.

2 packets plus 1³/₄ teaspoons unflavored gelatin

½ cup cranberry juice cocktail

1¼ pounds (4 to 5 medium) ripe peaches, peeled, pitted, and coarsely sliced

1 pound (about 3½ cups) coarsely sliced fresh strawberries

3 large egg whites

1 cup plus 2 tablespoons granulated sugar (or a little more if berries or peaches are very tart)

¼ cup heavy (whipping) cream

1 (10-ounce) package frozen raspberries in syrup, thawed

1½ to 2 cups small whole strawberries and peach slices, for filling center of ring or garnishing Bavarian sides

Makes 9 to 11 servings.

Oil a 2½-quart decorative ring mold, nonreactive Bundt pan, or other similar mold. Sprinkle gelatin over cranberry juice cocktail in a large saucepan; let stand for 5 minutes until softened. Add peach slices to gelatin mixture. Bring to a gentle simmer over medium heat, stirring until gelatin dissolves. Cover and gently simmer for 3 to 4 minutes, stirring frequently, until peaches are just barely tender. Remove pan from heat.

Transfer peach mixture to a blender. Blend until smooth. Add strawberries and blend several minutes

longer, until completely smooth. Refrigerate, stirring occasionally, until just cooled to room temperature.

Place egg whites in a large grease-free mixer bowl. Set mixer bowl in a larger bowl of very hot tap water. Let stand for 10 minutes, stirring frequently. Combine sugar and ¼ cup water in a medium saucepan, stirring until well blended. Bring to a simmer over medium-high heat. Cover and boil for 1½ minutes to allow steam to wash sugar from pan sides. Uncover and continue simmering, *without stirring,* for exactly 30 seconds longer. Immediately remove pan from heat.

Transfer mixer bowl to mixer and beat whites on medium speed until frothy and opaque. Raise speed to high and beat just until whites begin to form soft peaks; turn off mixer. Return hot syrup to burner and reheat just to boiling. Resume beating whites on high speed and immediately begin pouring hot syrup in a thin stream down bowl sides (avoid pouring syrup on beaters because it will stick to them). Pour rapidly enough that all syrup is incorporated in about 15 seconds. Continue beating on high speed until mixture is stiff, fluffy, and cooled to room temperature. Whisk peach-strawberry mixture into egg white mixture until smoothly incorporated.

In a mixer bowl with mixer set on high speed, beat

cream until soft peaks form. Whisk cream into fruit-egg white mixture until evenly incorporated. Turn out Bavarian into mold. Refrigerate, covered, for at least 5 hours and up to 24 hours before serving.

To prepare melba sauce, press raspberries and their syrup through a very fine sieve into a bowl; discard seeds. Cover and refrigerate for up to 24 hours before serving.

To serve, dip mold into hot water for 8 to 10 sec-onds and unmold on a rimmed platter. Fill center with strawberries and peach slices (or if solid mold was used place fruit around sides). If desired, pool a third of melba sauce around Bavarian and serve remainder separately in a small sauceboat.

Per serving (based on 11 servings):
Calories: 181   Grams of fat: 2.3   Grams of saturated fat: 1.3
Mgrams cholesterol: 7   Mgrams sodium: 20
Percentage of calories from fat: 11

lemon chiffon mousse with berry sauce

*A*iry and zesty, this smooth molded mousse makes a refreshing and attractive warm-weather dessert. It is served on a pool of either raspberry or blackberry sauce, both of which have an intense fruitiness and vivid color that complement the lemon beautifully. The mousse can be garnished with fresh fruits, or strewn with candied lemon zest shreds, if desired. ⌒ The mousse serves as the filling for the Charlotte Royale (pages 84–86).

½ cup (about 4 large) egg whites, completely free of yolk

¾ cup plus 2 tablespoons granulated sugar

3 tablespoons light corn syrup

½ cup fresh orange juice

1 envelope plus ¼ teaspoon unflavored gelatin

6½ tablespoons fresh lemon juice

1½ teaspoons *very finely* grated lemon zest (yellow part of skin)

⅓ cup heavy (whipping) cream

Berry Sauce and Optional Garnishes
Blackberry Sauce (page 127) *or* a double recipe Quick Raspberry Sauce (page 135)

2 cups assorted, very flavorful fruits, such as orange segments, pineapple chunks, tart plum slices, or blackberries

Candied lemon zest shreds (pages 136–37)

Makes 8 servings.

Lightly oil an 8-cup decorative mold (or 8 individual 1-cup molds, if preferred).

Place egg whites in a large grease-free mixer bowl. Set in a larger bowl of very hot tap water. Let stand for 10 minutes, stirring occasionally.

Combine sugar, corn syrup, and 3 tablespoons water in a 1-quart saucepan, stirring until well blended. Bring to a simmer over medium-high heat. Cover and boil for 1½ minutes to allow steam to wash any sugar from pan sides. Uncover and continue simmering, *without stirring*, for exactly 30 seconds longer. Immediately remove pan from heat.

Transfer mixer bowl holding egg whites to mixer. Beat whites on medium speed until frothy and opaque. Raise speed to high and beat until whites just begin to form peaks; do not overbeat. Immediately turn off mixer. Return hot syrup to burner and reheat just to a *full boil.* Beating whites on high speed, immediately begin pouring syrup in a thin stream down bowl sides (avoid pouring on beaters or syrup will stick to them or spin around bowl); pour rapidly so that all syrup is incorporated in about 15 seconds. Continue beating on high speed until meringue mixture stiffens, becomes fluffy, and cools to room temperature, several minutes longer. Cover and place in freezer while remaining ingredients are prepared.

Sprinkle orange juice over gelatin in a small saucepan. Set aside until gelatin softens, about 5 minutes. Place over medium heat and heat, stirring, until gelatin dissolves. Immediately remove pan from heat. Stir in lemon juice and zest. Set aside while cream is pre-pared. In a mixer bowl with mixer set on high speed, beat whipped cream until mixture stands in firm peaks.

Turn out gelatin mixture into a medium bowl. Set in a larger bowl of ice. Whisk mixture until it begins to thicken and jell. Immediately whisk it into cooled meringue until evenly incorporated. Then whisk whipped cream into meringue until well blended. Turn out mousse into mold (or individual molds). Cover and refrigerate for at least 5 hours and up to 24 hours, if preferred.

To unmold and serve mousse: Dip large mold in hot water for about 8 to 10 seconds or smaller individual molds for 4 to 5 seconds (don't overdo it). Run a knife around edges to loosen. Invert mousse onto serving platter (or individual molds onto dessert plates). Return to freezer briefly to firm up surface. Wipe platter clean around mousse. Pool half of sauce around mousse. Tuck optional fruit around sides *or* sprinkle top with candied lemon zest shreds. Cut into servings with a large knife. Pass remaining sauce separately. Alternatively, serve individual mousses on separate plates garnished with a pool of berry sauce (and optional fruits or candied zest, if desired).

Per serving (based on 8 servings):
Calories: 208   Grams of fat: 3.9   Grams of saturated fat: 2.3
Mgrams cholesterol: 14   Mgrams sodium: 38
Percentage of calories from fat: 16

Per serving (with fruit garnish):
Calories: 219   Grams of fat: 4   Grams of saturated fat: 2.3
Mgrams cholesterol: 14   Mgrams sodium: 39
Percentage of calories from fat: 16

trifle with blackberry sauce

*P*lump, succulent mixed fruit, smooth custard, a vibrant berry sauce, and plenty of cake to soak them all up are what trifles—and in this case dreams—are made of. Moreover, though it takes a bit of time to prepare the individual components of this classic British pudding, it can be put together well ahead of time. ➣ I can never decide whether I like this recipe or the Apricot Tipsy Parson with Meringue (pages 93–94) better. You might want to try them both.

1 recipe Blackberry Sauce (page 127)

1 tablespoon blackberry brandy or Grand Marnier (optional)

4¾ cups 1-inch cubes homemade or commercial angel food cake (a 12-ounce cake yields about the right amount)

1¼ cups halved strawberries

1¼ cups fresh pineapple chunks

1 cup peeled and coarsely sliced peaches tossed with 1 teaspoon lemon juice

1 cup sliced bananas, tossed with 1 teaspoon lemon juice

1 cup mixed fresh fruit, such as green and red seedless grapes, peeled and coarsely cubed kiwi fruit, blackberries, or red raspberries

A *double recipe* of Brandied Orange Custard Cream (page 151)

½ cup blackberries, raspberries, or small, whole strawberries, or a combination, for garnish (optional)

Fresh mint sprigs, for garnish (optional)

Makes 9 or 10 servings.

Combine blackberry sauce with brandy (if used). Drizzle a third of blackberry sauce in a 2-quart glass trifle bowl or similar attractive glass serving bowl. Arrange half of cake cubes over sauce, patting down slightly. Arrange half of the strawberry halves, pineapple chunks, peach and banana slices, and mixed fruit over cake, pressing an occasional piece of fruit flat against the glass. Spread half of custard cream over fruit. Add another third of blackberry sauce, then remainder of cake, patting it down lightly. Place remaining strawberries, pineapple, peaches, bananas, and mixed fruit over cake. Top fruit with remaining blackberry sauce. Spread last of custard over top. Cover and chill for at least 1 hour, and up to 18 hours, if desired.

If desired, garnish top of trifle with fresh berries and mint sprigs. Spoon trifle into individual dishes and serve.

Per serving (based on 10 servings):
Calories: 288 Grams of fat: 3.8 Grams of saturated fat: 1.8
Mgrams cholesterol: 51 Mgrams sodium: 113
Percentage of calories from fat: 11

maple-glazed maple custard

*T*his dessert is similar to the classic French favorite, Crème Caramel, but with a wonderful American twist. Instead of being lined with caramel, the custard cups are coated with a boiled-down maple syrup glaze. To intensify the flavor even more, maple syrup is substituted for sugar in the custard mixture.

Maple Glaze
½ cup maple syrup
1 tablespoon light corn syrup

Custard and Optional Garnish
1¼ cups 2-percent fat milk
1 cup whole milk
1 (3-inch) piece vanilla bean (see Note)
Pinch of salt
2 large eggs plus 2 large egg whites
⅓ cup maple syrup
3 tablespoons Maple-Pecan Praline (page 140), optional

Makes 6 servings.

Preheat oven to 350° F. Set 6 custard cups or heat-proof ¾- to 1-cup ramekins in a pan large enough to hold them. Warm the cups by adding ½ inch very hot water to pan. Fill a heatproof cup with cold water; and add several ice cubes.

To prepare maple glaze: In a 1-quart saucepan over medium-high heat, bring maple syrup and corn syrup to a simmer. Reduce heat and simmer, lifting pan and gently swirling occasionally (but never stirring), for 3 minutes. Begin testing syrup for doneness by

dropping ½ teaspoon into ice water. If syrup forms a hard, almost brittle ball when squeezed, it is done; immediately lift pan from heat. Working carefully (mixture is extremely hot) and dividing syrup among the cups, pour a tablespoon into each one, immediately tipping cup from side to side to coat entire bottom surface. Set coated cups aside to allow maple glaze to cool and firm. (If mixture stiffens as you divide it among cups, reheat until fluid and then continue.)

To prepare custard: In a medium saucepan over medium-high heat, bring 2-percent and whole milk, vanilla bean, and salt just to a simmer. Remove from heat and set aside to cool to barely hot. In a medium-sized bowl, beat eggs and whites and maple syrup with a fork, until well blended. Remove vanilla bean from milk. Beating with a fork, add about a third of milk to egg mixture; then slowly beat remaining milk into egg mixture. Strain mixture through a fine sieve and divide among prepared cups. Return cups to pan and transfer to lower rack of oven.

Add enough hot water to reach halfway up sides of cups. Bake for 25 to 35 minutes, or just until custards appear set when cups are jiggled. Remove cups to wire racks and let stand to cool. Refrigerate until chilled, at least 1 hour (and up to 3 days), before serving; maple glaze thins out a bit after a few hours but tastes just the same. Run a knife around custards to loosen, then invert onto serving plates. Sprinkle each custard with ½ tablespoon praline, if desired. Serve immediately.

Note: If vanilla bean is unavailable, substitute 2¼ teaspoons vanilla extract. Add when eggs and whites are added.

Per serving (based on 6 servings):
Calories: 207   Grams of fat: 4   Grams of saturated fat: 2
Mgrams cholesterol: 80   Mgrams sodium: 159
Percentage of calories from fat: 17

Per serving (with praline garnish):
Calories: 238   Grams of fat: 5.2   Grams of saturated fat: 2
Mgrams cholesterol: 80   Mgrams sodium: 159
Percentage of calories from fat: 19

apricot tipsy parson with meringue

*R*oughly adapted from a recipe by James Beard, this pretty, meringue-topped tipsy parson delivers the same sublime amalgam of apricot, almond, custard, and sherry-soaked sponge cake as the original, but does so with a fraction of the fat. (Beard's recipe called for twice as many egg yolks and 2 cups of heavy cream compared to 2 tablespoons in this slimmed-down version.) Nevertheless, this traditional English dessert—which originally got its name from its potential for making the person eating it tipsy—tastes absolutely luxurious! ～ Like the Trifle with Blackberry Sauce (page 91), this fancy pudding makes a fine company dessert.

1 recipe Lemon Roulade, pages 144–45 (prepared as directed, except left unrolled)

About 1 tablespoon powdered sugar, for dusting cake surface

1 recipe Apricot Sauce (page 131), well chilled

⅓ cup Amaretti cookie crumbs

¼ cup cream sherry

A *double recipe* of Brandied Orange Custard Cream (page 151)

Meringue and Garnish

½ cup egg whites, completely free of yolk and at room temperature

½ teaspoon cream of tartar

Pinch of salt

Generous ½ cup granulated sugar

½ teaspoon vanilla extract

3 drops almond extract

1 or 2 diced dried apricots, for garnish (optional)

Makes 8 to 10 servings.

If cake is freshly baked, allow to cool thoroughly. Peel off paper and allow cake to stand, uncovered, on wire rack for 30 minutes to dry out. Cut in half crosswise.

Lay half on cutting board. Dust surface of cake with powdered sugar. Lay second half over first. Cut into ¾-inch cubes using a serrated knife; if necessary, wipe knife clean several times as you work. Set cubes aside.

Set out a 7½- by 12-inch glass baking dish or similarly-sized decorative ovenproof glass casserole. Spread a third of apricot sauce evenly in bottom of baking dish. Sprinkle with half of Amaretti crumbs. Cover with half of cake cubes, patting down to compress slightly. Sprinkle with half of sherry. Top cake with half of custard cream. Spread on another third of apricot sauce. Sprinkle over remainder of Amaretti crumbs. Cover with remaining cake cubes. Sprinkle remaining sherry over cake. Top cake with remaining custard. Top with remainder of apricot sauce. Cover and refrigerate mixture until thoroughly chilled, at least 2½ hours and up to 12 hours, if desired.

Prepare meringue: Preheat oven to 350° F. In a completely grease-free mixing bowl with mixer set on medium speed, beat egg whites and cream of tartar until frothy. Add salt and continue beating *just until very soft peaks begin forming.* Immediately add granulated sugar, about a tablespoon at a time, then vanilla and almond extracts, continuing to beat on medium speed until mixture is smooth and stands in soft, fluffy peaks. Spoon mixture into a pastry bag fitted with a ½-inch diameter plain tip. Pipe meringue over surface of tipsy parson, being sure entire surface is covered out to edge of dish. (Alternatively, spoon dollops of mixture over surface and spread out and swirl with a table knife.)

Bake in lower third of oven for 15 to 16 minutes, or until meringue is well browned and looks set. Garnish top with diced dried apricots, if desired. Serve tipsy parson immediately or return to refrigerator and chill for up to 6 hours, if preferred.

Per serving (based on 10 servings):
Calories: 341   Grams of fat: 4.7   Grams of saturated fat: 2.1
Mgrams cholesterol: 93   Mgrams sodium: 187
Percentage of calories from fat: 12

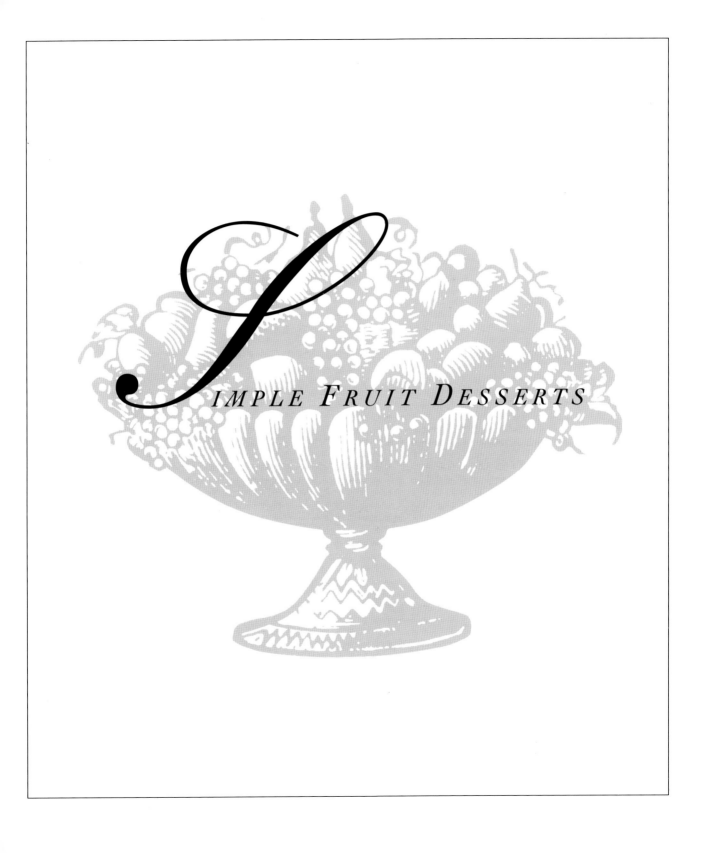

SIMPLE FRUIT DESSERTS

blueberry (or rhubarb-strawberry) cobbler

*P*lump with juicy fruit and mellowed with a biscuit crust, a warm, fragrant bowlful of cobbler is among the most rewarding of all desserts. ∿ This recipe makes either a blueberry or a rhubarb-and-strawberry cobbler (see directions for the latter on page 97). ∿ Though cobblers are as satisfying and substantial as pies, they are generally lower in fat, because a single crust is used and biscuit doughs tend to be less rich than pie doughs.

Filling

⅔ cup granulated sugar

2½ tablespoons cornstarch

⅛ teaspoon ground cinnamon

¼ cup cranberry juice cocktail

⅛ teaspoon finely grated lemon zest (yellow part of skin)

4 cups fresh or unsweetened frozen blueberries (if using frozen, rinse and drain well first)

½ teaspoon unsalted butter

Dough and Garnish

1⅓ cups all-purpose flour

1½ tablespoons granulated sugar

½ teaspoon baking powder

¼ teaspoon salt

2 tablespoons cold Browned Butter (page 147) or unsalted butter, cut into small pieces

1 tablespoon canola or safflower oil

5 tablespoons skim milk

2 teaspoons fresh lemon juice

Small scoops (¼ cup) of light ice cream or ice milk, for garnish (optional)

Makes 5 or 6 servings.

Preheat oven to 375° F. Set out a 2-quart or similar-size ovenproof casserole.

For filling: In a 2-quart saucepan, thoroughly stir together sugar, cornstarch, and cinnamon. Slowly stir in cranberry juice and lemon zest until well blended and smooth. Add blueberries and butter. Heat mixture over medium heat, stirring, for about 3 minutes, or until bubbly, thickened slightly, and clear. Turn out mixture into casserole.

For dough: In a medium-sized bowl, thoroughly stir together flour, sugar, baking powder, and salt. Add butter and oil to flour mixture. Using a pastry blender, forks, or your fingertips, cut in butter and oil, until mixture resembles coarse meal. Stir together milk and lemon juice in a measuring cup. Add to flour mixture, tossing with a fork just until evenly incorporated. Pat mixture into a ball. Lay between sheets of wax paper and press into a round almost large enough to top the fruit filling. Peel off one sheet of paper. If desired, pinch edge of pastry all the way around to create a scalloped effect. Center dough, wax paper-side up, over fruit mixture. Peel off and discard second sheet of paper. Make several 1½-inch-long decorative slashes radiating from center of dough top.

Rhubarb-Strawberry Cobbler

Bake in preheated oven for 35 to 45 minutes, or until top is nicely browned and a toothpick inserted in the center comes out clean. Let cool for at least 10 minutes before serving.

Spoon into bowls and garnish with light ice cream, if desired. Cobbler may also be refrigerated, covered, for up to 3 days and reheated in a 300° F. oven just before serving.

Variation: Rhubarb-Strawberry Cobbler

Substitute 2 2/3 cups of 3/4-inch pieces fresh rhubarb and 1 1/2 cups halved fresh strawberries for blueberries. Increase cranberry juice cocktail to 1/3 cup and sugar to 3/4 cup plus 2 tablespoons.

To prepare fruit, combine dry ingredients and add cranberry juice and lemon zest as directed. Then add rhubarb and butter and cook for 3 to 4 minutes.

Remove from heat and stir in strawberries. Proceed exactly as directed.

Per serving (Blueberry—based on 6 servings):
Calories: 317   Grams of fat: 7.3   Grams of saturated fat: 3
Mgrams cholesterol: 12   Mgrams sodium: 131
Percentage of calories from fat: 20

Per serving (with light ice cream):
Calories: 373   Grams of fat: 8.4   Grams of saturated fat: 3.7
Mgrams cholesterol: 15   Mgrams sodium: 172
Percentage of calories from fat: 20

Per serving (Rhubarb-Strawberry—based on 6 servings):
Calories: 317   Grams of fat: 7.1   Grams of saturated fat: 3
Mgrams cholesterol: 12   Mgrams sodium: 129
Percentage of calories from fat: 20

Per serving (with light ice cream):
Calories: 372   Grams of fat: 8.3   Grams of saturated fat: 3.7
Mgrams cholesterol: 15   Mgrams sodium: 169
Percentage of calories from fat: 19

sautéed pears with light ice cream & caramel

*T*hough pears and chocolate are a better known combination than pears and caramel, I think the latter choice is more enticing. Rather than overpowering the subtle flavor of the fruit, the caramel simply mingles with and enriches it. Moreover, pears have just enough acid to balance the ultra-sweet taste of caramel sauce. ⌣ Add to the warm pears and gooey caramel a scoop of cold, creamy, light ice cream and perhaps a sprinkling of crunchy almond praline for textural contrast and you have a "simple" fruit dessert that is much more than the sum of its parts.

6 medium-sized, slightly under-ripe Anjou or Bartlett pears, peeled, halved, and cored

2 tablespoons lemon juice combined with 2 cups water

1/3 cup granulated sugar

1/2 tablespoon unsalted butter, cut into pieces

1 teaspoon vanilla extract

6 scoops (1/2 cup) vanilla light ice cream or ice milk

1 recipe Caramel Sauce (pages 134–35), at room temperature or slightly warm

3 tablespoons Almond Praline (pages 138–40), optional

Makes 6 servings.

To prevent fruit from discoloring, stir together pears and lemon-water in a nonreactive bowl. Turn out pears into a colander; drain well.

Place sugar and butter in a 12-inch nonreactive metal skillet or sauté pan (see Note). Spread pears over sugar, stirring to coat. Place over medium-high heat and heat, stirring with a long-handled wooden spoon, until butter melts and pears begin to release juice.

Raise heat to high and continue cooking, stirring occasionally, for 4 to 7 minutes longer, until pears are lightly caramelized and almost tender when pierced with a fork; do not overcook. Using a slotted spoon, transfer pears to a colander set over a bowl. Let stand for 10 minutes. Add juice that has accumulated from pears to skillet. Adjust heat as needed so mixture in skillet *bubbles vigorously and syrup boils down and thickens just slightly but does not turn brown or burn.* Remove pan from heat and stir in vanilla. At this point, the mixture may be set aside, covered, for up to 2 hours, if desired.

To assemble desserts, using a slotted spoon, return pears to the skillet. Place over medium heat and gently toss the pears until coated with syrup and warmed. Place a scoop of light ice cream on each serving plate or dish. Tuck 2 pear halves, core side in, around each ice cream scoop. Drizzle each dessert with Caramel

Sauce. Sprinkle each with ½ tablespoon almond praline, if desired, and serve immediately.

Note: Be sure to use a nonreactive skillet, such as stainless steel, enamel-coated cast iron, or nonstick-clad (such as Teflon). Avoid plain cast iron or aluminum, which can react with the acid in the pears and lend a tinny taste.

Per serving (based on 6 servings):
Calories: 398   Grams of fat: 6.8   Grams of saturated fat: 3.8
Mgrams cholesterol: 19   Mgrams sodium: 142
Percentage of calories from fat: 15

Per serving (with Almond Praline):
Calories: 421   Grams of fat: 7.6   Grams of saturated fat: 3.9
Mgrams cholesterol: 19   Mgrams sodium: 142
Percentage of calories from fat: 16

glazed orange slices

$\mathcal{I}$ cannot think of any other fruit dessert that, spoonful for spoonful, delivers so much glorious flavor, vibrant color, and enticing aroma. Since the oranges are not only delicious but nearly fat-free and rich in vitamin C, it is possible to feel both self-indulgent and self-righteous when you eat them! ⌁ Served alone, or perhaps with a light, crisp cookie, glazed orange slices make a perfect ending to a heavy meal.

6 flavorful, brightly colored oranges, preferably navel

1 piece (1-inch long) fresh ginger root with a quarter-size diameter, peeled

⅓ cup granulated sugar

2 tablespoons light corn syrup

3 tablespoons Grand Marnier (or substitute orange juice, if preferred)

Mint sprigs, for garnish (optional)

Makes 5 or 6 servings.

Using a vegetable peeler, peel strips of zest from 1½ oranges; be careful to remove only orange layer and no white pith. Using a paring knife, cut strips of zest into very fine matchstick-length shreds. Combine zest strips and 1 cup water in a medium-sized saucepan over medium-high heat. Bring to a boil and cook for 3 minutes. Turn out zest into a sieve. Rinse zest under cool water; let drain.

Using a sharp knife, remove peel and all pith from oranges. Cut oranges crosswise into ⅛-inch-thick slices and reserve in a nonreactive bowl. Refrigerate until chilled, at least 30 minutes, or up to 8 hours, if desired.

Rinse out saucepan and return zest strips to it. Using a paring knife, cut ginger into very thin matchstick shreds. Add ginger, sugar, corn syrup, and Grand Marnier to saucepan. Bring to a boil over medium-high heat. Adjust heat so mixture simmers gently and cook, stirring occasionally, for about 3 minutes, or until shreds of zest are tender and just translucent. Remove orange and ginger shreds with tines of a fork, spreading them out on a sheet of wax paper. Drain any juice from oranges into saucepan. Return pan to heat and continue simmering until mixture is slightly thickened and syrupy but not at all browned. Remove pan from heat and let stand until cooled almost to room temperature. If syrup is too stiff to drizzle, thin it with a few drops of water until fluid. Syrup may be used immediately, or refrigerated for up to 8 hours and then brought to room temperature before using.

To serve: Arrange a layer of orange slices in dessert dishes or cups. Drizzle top of slices with syrup. Sprinkle over a few candied orange and ginger shreds. Add another layer of slices and top with syrup and candied shreds, continuing until all oranges are used and glazed. Generously sprinkle more candied orange and ginger shreds over each serving. Garnish servings with mint sprigs, if desired.

Per serving (based on 6 servings):
Calories: 139   Grams of fat: 0.2   Grams of saturated fat: 0
Mgrams cholesterol: 0   Mgrams sodium: 5
Percentage of calories from fat: 1

autumn fruit compote

$\mathscr{T}$his compote can be served any time of year, but I think of it as the quintessential autumn dessert. Extraordinarily mellow, it brings together several dried fruits with a hint of spice, lemon, fruity white wine, and vanilla. ∽ If at all possible, use a vanilla bean rather than vanilla extract in this recipe. It lends a wonderful depth of flavor and a perfume that the extract does not.

1 cup (4 ounces) dried pears

1 cup (4 ounces) halved dried apricots, preferably American

²⁄₃ cup (3 ounces) dried pitted prunes

1³⁄₄ cup water

²⁄₃ cup fruity white wine, such as Rhine or Mosel

¹⁄₃ cup granulated sugar

2 teaspoons fresh lemon juice

2 (1-inch thick) lemon slices

¹⁄₈ teaspoon ground cinnamon

1 (2¹⁄₂-inch-long) piece vanilla bean, split in half lengthwise (see Note)

Dollops (3 tablespoons) of Fruit Crème (page 140) or low-fat vanilla yogurt, for garnish (optional)

Makes 5 or 6 servings.

Cut each pear into 4 lengthwise strips, removing and discarding the pithy center portions from each. Halve apricot halves and prunes.

Stir together fruit, 1³⁄₄ cup water, the wine, sugar, lemon juice and slices, cinnamon, and vanilla bean in a medium saucepan. Bring mixture to a simmer over medium-high heat. Lower heat and gently simmer for 10 to 12 minutes, or until fruit is tender and much of the liquid has been absorbed. Remove pan from heat. Let cool to warm. Discard lemon slices. Using a paring knife, scrape as much pulp as possible from the vanilla bean into compote. If storing fruit, return vanilla bean to it; discard vanilla bean just before serving. Compote may be stored, refrigerated, for up to 2 weeks. Serve at room temperature or just lightly chilled. Garnish servings with Fruit Crème or low-fat vanilla yogurt, if desired.

Note: If vanilla bean is unavailable, substitute 2 teaspoons vanilla extract. Add it when pan is removed from heat.

Per serving (based on 6 servings):
Calories: 234   Grams of fat: 0.4   Grams of sat. fat: 0
Mgrams cholesterol: 0   Mgrams sodium: 6
Percentage of calories from fat: 1

Per serving (with Fruit Crème):
Calories: 302   Grams of fat: 2.4   Grams of sat. fat: 1.2
Mgrams cholesterol: 7   Mgrams sodium: 41
Percentage of calories from fat: 7

Raspberry-Fruit Gratins

raspberry-fruit gratin

*F*resh fruit gratins are at once elegant and simple. In this version, fruit slices and raspberries are arranged in individual gratin dishes, blanketed with a whipped cream–custard sauce, dusted with powdered sugar, and then run under a broiler just until the surface is bubbly-brown. The resulting interplay of flavor, texture, and fragrance is pure heaven. ⌣ If you cannot find the exact assortment of fruits called for here, just fill in with whatever flavorful, succulent choices are available. Try not to omit the raspberries, however—they are particularly irresistible in this dessert.

1 recipe Brandied Orange Custard Cream (page 151),
    prepared as directed *except omit the heavy cream*
    (at room temperature)

¼ cup well-chilled heavy (whipping) cream

2 large, ripe nectarines *or* 1 peeled large, ripe mango,
    coarsely sliced

6 very ripe (¼-inch-thick) fresh pineapple slices, quartered

1 large banana, cut on a diagonal into ¼-inch-thick
    crosswise slices

1 very ripe kiwi fruit, peeled and cut crosswise into rounds
    and then cut again into half slices

1 cup fresh red raspberries

About 2 tablespoons powdered sugar

Makes 6 servings.

Lightly grease six 6½-inch round or similar oven-proof gratin dishes. Preheat broiler at highest heat.

Whisk orange custard until smooth and well blended. Place heavy cream in a mixer bowl. With mixer on high speed, beat cream just to firm peaks. Whisk orange custard into whipped cream until well blended and smooth. Divide fruit and berries among dishes, arranging pieces attractively. Divide orange cream mixture among dishes, spreading it attractively over the fruit. (These dishes can be prepared and then refrigerated, covered, for up to 4 hours, if desired.)

Just before serving, sift about a teaspoon of powdered sugar over each gratin. Immediately place gratin dishes in preheated broiler about 4 inches from heating element and broil for 2 to 3 minutes, or until orange cream mixture is bubbly and lightly browned. Remove gratins from oven and serve immediately.

Per serving (based on 6 servings):
Calories: 187   Grams of fat: 5.2   Grams of saturated fat: 2.6
Mgrams cholesterol: 50   Mgrams sodium: 20
Percentage of calories from fat: 24

berry-apple pudding cake

*S*imilar to a cobbler but less rich, this homey baked dessert features the zesty, flavorful combination of apples and either blackberries or raspberries. I first devised the berry-apple blend to stretch several cups of black raspberries I'd gathered while foraging, then liked the combination so much I made the recipe part of my regular repertoire. Fresh blackberries or red or black raspberries can all be used in this recipe. On several occasions when I yearned for the taste of summer and there were no fresh berries to be had, I even substituted frozen berries with success.

Scant ⅔ cup granulated sugar

1 tablespoon cornstarch

¼ teaspoon ground cinnamon

1¾ cups (about 2 medium) peeled and chopped tart cooking apples, such as Granny Smith

1½ tablespoons fresh lemon juice

2¾ cups fresh or frozen (unsweetened) blackberries or red or black raspberries

Batter

1¼ cups all-purpose flour

1½ teaspoons baking powder

¼ teaspoon salt

¼ teaspoon ground cinnamon

½ cup granulated sugar

2 tablespoons Browned Butter (page 147) or unsalted butter, slightly softened

1½ tablespoons canola or safflower oil

1 large egg white

1¼ teaspoons vanilla extract

½ teaspoon finely grated lemon zest (yellow part of skin)

⅔ cup skim milk

Small scoops (⅓ cup) ice milk or fat-free ice cream, for garnish (optional)

Makes 7 or 8 servings.

Preheat oven to 350° F. Lightly grease (or spray with nonstick vegetable oil spray) a 7½- by 13-inch or similar flat baking dish.

Stir together sugar, cornstarch, and cinnamon in a 2-quart saucepan. Stir in apples and lemon juice until incorporated. Bring mixture to a simmer, stirring, over medium heat. Simmer, uncovered and stirring occasionally, for 5 minutes. Stir in berries and simmer just until they release their juices. Set aside.

To prepare batter: In a medium-sized bowl, thoroughly stir together flour, baking powder, salt and cinnamon. In a mixing bowl with mixer on medium speed, beat sugar, butter, and oil, until smooth and well blended. Beat in egg white, vanilla, and lemon zest. Gently fold in half of dry ingredients. Lightly stir in milk, then remainder of flour mixture, just until thoroughly incorporated but not overmixed.

Immediately spread batter evenly in pan. Evenly pour berry-apple mixture over batter; do not stir.

Bake cake in center third of oven for 25 minutes. Lower temperature to 325° F. and continue baking for 10 minutes longer, or until fruit is bubbly and a toothpick inserted in cake center comes out clean. Let cool on wire rack for 5 minutes. Serve spooned into bowls, along with small scoops of ice milk or fat-free ice cream, if desired.

Pudding cake will keep, covered, for up to 48 hours. Serve warm or at room temperature.

Per serving (based on 8 servings):
Calories: 277   Grams of fat: 6.1   Grams of saturated fat: 2.2
Mgrams cholesterol: 8   Mgrams sodium: 147
Percentage of calories from fat: 19

Per serving (served with ice milk):
Calories: 369   Grams of fat: 8.9   Grams of saturated fat: 3.9
Mgrams cholesterol: 17   Mgrams sodium: 199
Percentage of calories from fat: 21

Per serving (served with fat-free ice cream):
Calories: 382   Grams of fat: 6.1   Grams of saturated fat: 2.2
Mgrams cholesterol: 19   Mgrams sodium: 213
Percentage of calories from fat: 14

brown sugar–glazed broiled pineapple with raspberries

*B*rown sugar and pineapple have a great affinity for one another, and the pairing seems even more wonderful when the two are lightly caramelized during broiling. The raspberries are not really cooked in this recipe—just warmed and glazed in the bubbly, sugary juice left after the pineapple is broiled. The entire dessert takes less than 10 minutes to prepare. ∼ For fullest flavor, use the ripest (usually the yellowest), most fragrant pineapple you can find.

3 tablespoons packed dark brown sugar
1 teaspoon Browned Butter (page 147) or unsalted butter, softened
1 teaspoon light rum (or substitute orange juice, if preferred)
¼ teaspoon vanilla extract
6 very ripe (¼-inch thick) fresh pineapple slices, halved
½ cup fresh red raspberries

Makes 4 generous servings or 6 small servings.

Lightly grease a 7½- by 11-inch shallow glass baking dish. Preheat broiler at highest heat.

In a small heatproof bowl, stir together brown sugar, butter, rum, and vanilla. Place in a microwave oven, loosely covered with wax paper, and microwave on high power until butter melts and mixture is bubbly, about 30 seconds. Immediately remove from oven and stir briefly. (Alternatively, place mixture in a small saucepan and heat over medium heat until bubbly. Immediately remove from heat.)

Using a pastry brush or table knife, very lightly brush pineapple half slices with brown sugar mixture. Arrange, glaze-side down and slightly separated, in prepared baking dish. Place dish about 4 inches from heating element and broil for about 2 minutes, or until slices are hot and edges are bubbly. Remove from broiler and evenly brush tops of slices with remaining brown sugar mixture. Return to oven and broil for about 40 to 60 seconds longer, until brown sugar is bubbling all over but is not burned. Divide pineapple slices among serving dishes, arranging sugar-side up. Toss raspberries into brown-sugar mixture remaining in bottom of baking dish until evenly coated. Return berries to broiler and heat for 10 to 15 seconds, watching carefully, just until heated through but not at all cooked or soft. Sprinkle raspberries over pineapple and serve immediately.

Per serving (based on 6 servings):
Calories: 52   Grams of fat: 0.8   Grams of saturated fat: 0.4
Mgrams cholesterol: 2   Mgrams sodium: 2
Percentage of calories from fat: 14

fruit & berry salad with vanilla bean sauce

*I*n this lovely dessert salad, kiwis are an essential element, providing not only color, but also a crunch that plays up the texture of the vanilla bean seeds and a taste that is surprisingly rich and pleasing. Be sure the kiwi fruits are completely ripe; they should give slightly when pressed with a finger. ➤ The berries are another important part of this dessert, though if all three kinds are not in the market at once, you can substitute a generous cup of each of two varieties. If available, plump, sweet blackberries should definitely be included. ➤ Unlike many fruit salads, this one is best served just barely chilled. Also, the fruits should be kept separate until serving time so that each retains its unique character and can be individually savored with the sauce. For a more substantial dessert, a very small scoop of Easy Raspberry Ice may be spooned alongside the fruits.

Sauce
2 ½ tablespoons sieved apricot preserves
1 tablespoon granulated sugar

1 (3-inch) piece vanilla bean, split lengthwise
1 teaspoon fresh orange juice
1 teaspoon fresh lemon juice

Fruit and Optional Garnish

3 fully ripe kiwi fruits, peeled and cut in eighths lengthwise

1 very large, flavorful orange, peeled, segmented (with segments membrane-free) and well drained

¾ cup very ripe (⅛-inch thick) pineapple chunks, well drained

¾ cup fresh red raspberries

¾ cup fresh blackberries

¾ cup halved strawberries

Very small scoops (2 tablespoons) of Easy Raspberry Ice (pages 119–21), optional

Makes 5 or 6 servings.

Combine apricot preserves, sugar, vanilla bean, orange juice, and ¾ cup water in a 1-quart saucepan. Bring to a boil over medium-high heat. Reduce heat so mixture simmers gently and cook for 4 to 5 minutes, or until sauce is reduced to a scant ½ cup. Remove pan from heat. Stir in lemon juice. Using a small paring knife, scrape seeds from pieces of vanilla bean into sauce. Return vanilla bean pieces to sauce. Set sauce aside to cool to room temperature. Use imme-diately or cover and refrigerate for up to 4 days and then return to room temperature before using.

Up to 4 hours before serving time, ready fruits, keeping each kind separate. Use immediately or refrigerate and then bring back to room temperature before using.

To assemble salads: Dividing equally, attractively arrange some of each kind of fruit and berry on 5 or 6 dessert plates. Remove vanilla bean pieces from vanilla sauce. Sauce should be slightly thickened but still fluid enough to drizzle; thin it with a few drops of water, if necessary. Drizzle a tablespoon of vanilla sauce over each salad. If desired, garnish each salad with Raspberry Ice. Serve immediately.

Per serving (based on 6 servings):
Calories: 96   Grams of fat: 0.5   Grams of saturated fat: 0
Mgrams cholesterol: 0   Mgrams sodium: 4
Percentage of calories from fat: 4

Per serving (with Raspberry Ice):
Calories: 177   Grams of fat: 0.6   Grams of saturated fat: 0
Mgrams cholesterol: 50   Mgrams sodium: 9
Percentage of calories from fat: 3

cranberry-apple (or blueberry-apple) crumble

*T*he name "crumble" *sounds* like a casual, home-style dish, and it is. Here, you have your choice between the slightly tart, tangy combination of cranberry and apple, or the mellower, sweeter blueberry-apple blend; see the variation (photograph at right). The cranberries need more sugaring, but beyond that the two versions are prepared in exactly the same way.

¾ cup rolled oats

¾ cup packed light or dark brown sugar

3 tablespoons all-purpose flour

½ teaspoon ground cinnamon

2 tablespoons chilled Browned Butter (page 147) or
    unsalted butter

1½ tablespoons canola or safflower oil

3⅔ cups (4 to 5 medium) peeled and finely sliced Stamen,
    Rome, or other cooking apples

1 tablespoon lemon juice

¼ teaspoon finely grated lemon zest (yellow part of skin)

2⅔ cups fresh or frozen (thawed) unsweetened cranberries,
    coarsely chopped

Small scoops (¼ cup) of vanilla light ice cream or ice milk,
    for garnish (optional)

Makes 5 or 6 servings.

Preheat oven to 375° F. Lightly grease a 7½- by 11-inch baking dish or round dish with similar volume.

Stir together oats, brown sugar, flour and cinnamon. Using forks or your fingertips, cut in butter and oil until thoroughly incorporated. Set mixture aside.

In a large bowl, toss apples with lemon juice and zest until well combined. Stir in cranberries. Reserve scant 1 cup oat mixture for topping. Add remainder of oat mixture to fruit, tossing until well mixed. Spread mixture in baking dish. Sprinkle reserved oat mixture over top.

Bake for 35 to 45 minutes, or until mixture is bubbly and nicely browned on top and apples in center are tender when pierced with a fork. Transfer to a cooling rack. Crumble may be served warm or at room temperature, plain or with light ice cream. Store, refrigerated, for up to 3 days.

Variation: Blueberry-Apple Crumble

Reduce sugar to 6 or 7 tablespoons (use larger amount for very tart blueberries). Substitute 2⅔ cups fresh or frozen unsweetened *whole* blueberries for cranberries.

Per serving (Cranberry-Apple—based on 6 servings):
Calories: 323   Grams of fat: 9.2   Grams of saturated fat: 3
Mgrams cholesterol: 11   Mgrams sodium: 10
Percentage of calories from fat: 25

Per serving (with light ice cream):
Calories: 379   Grams of fat: 10.3   Grams of saturated fat: 3.8
Mgrams cholesterol: 14   Mgrams sodium: 50
Percentage of calories from fat: 24

Per serving (Blueberry-Apple—based on 6 servings):
Calories: 284   Grams of fat: 9.3   Grams of saturated fat: 3.8
Mgrams cholesterol: 11   Mgrams sodium: 9
Percentage of calories from fat: 28

Per serving (with light ice cream):
Calories: 340   Grams of fat: 10.5   Grams of saturated fat: 3.8
Mgrams cholesterol: 14   Mgrams sodium: 50
Percentage of calories from fat: 27

SIMPLE FRUIT DESSERTS

peach melba meringues

*V*anilla meringue shells are a boon on occasions when a plain fruit dessert seems too insubstantial, but dietary fat must be minimized. Almost instantly, they can be paired with fresh fruit to yield sumptuous, satisfying, and virtually fat-free desserts—that also happen to look quite pretty. ∼ In the following recipe, the meringue shells are served with peaches and raspberries, light vanilla ice cream, and a drizzling of raspberry sauce. Heavenly, easy, and only 2.6 grams of fat apiece.

4 large ripe peaches

1 teaspoon fresh lemon juice

1½ tablespoons granulated sugar, or more to taste

1 recipe Meringues (pages 142–44), thoroughly cooled

Small scoops (½ cup) of vanilla light ice cream or
   ice milk

1 cup red raspberries or sliced strawberries, or a
   combination of the two

1 recipe Quick Raspberry Sauce (page 135),
   well chilled

Makes 8 servings.

About 15 minutes before serving time, peel and slice peaches and toss with lemon juice and sugar in a nonreactive bowl. Cover and refrigerate until lightly chilled.

Arrange meringues on individual dessert plates. Top each with small scoop of ice cream. Gently stir berries into peaches. Spoon fruit over meringues, dividing equally among them. Drizzle Raspberry Sauce over each dessert and serve immediately.

Per serving (based on 8 servings):
Calories: 285   Grams of fat: 2.6   Grams of saturated fat: 1.4
Mgrams cholesterol: 6   Mgrams sodium: 143
Percentage of calories from fat: 8

SIMPLE FRUIT DESSERTS

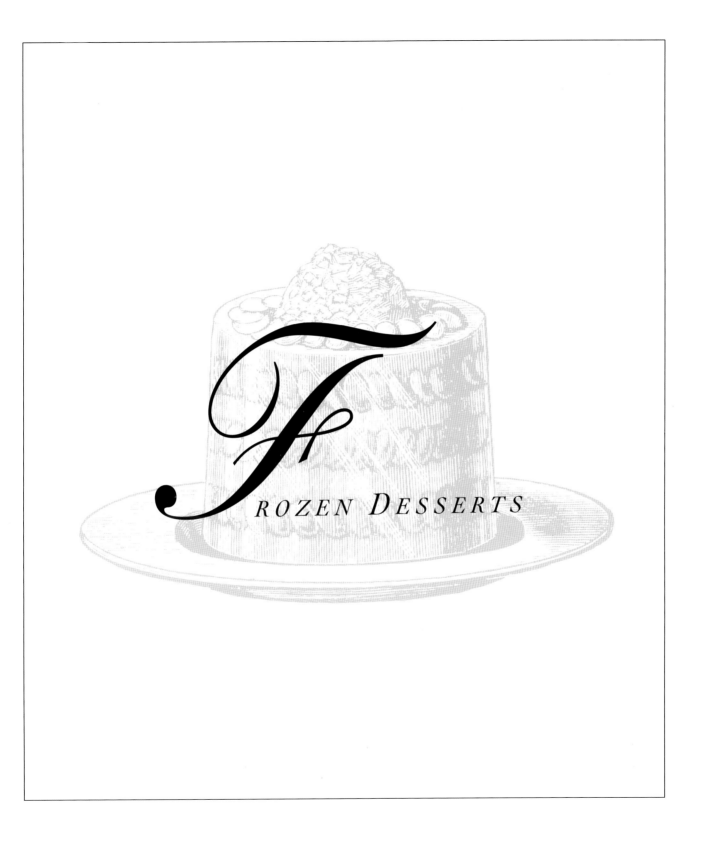

FROZEN DESSERTS

watermelon sorbet

$\mathcal{F}$or years, I tried to create a sorbet that captured the very essence of ripe summer watermelon, but my attempts always fell a little short. Finally, however, I hit the mark—fresh, unsullied watermelon taste, only better. ∾ One major problem with watermelon is its naturally high water content. Adding even small amounts of liquid can dilute its flavor and color, yet *some* liquid must normally be added in the process of transforming a fruit into sorbet. Also, intensifying the natural flavor is trickier with watermelon than with most fruits because its delicate taste can easily be overpowered by the usual enhancers (such as lemon zest or juice or spices). ∾ Here, the solution to both problems is cranberry juice concentrate. Its acidity and intense fruitiness help bring out the watermelon flavor without overwhelming it. As a bonus, the vivid cranberry color adds depth to the already pretty watermelon shade. Along with the cranberry, I sometimes add a hint of ginger, which lends an aromatic, faintly exotic cast. ∾ Though this sorbet is attractive served "as is," it is striking tucked back into an empty watermelon rind and served cut into slices as fresh watermelon would be. This makes a great company presentation, as the slices can be prepared well ahead; see the directions for this variation at the end of the recipe.

3¼ cups (scant 1¼ pounds) seeded, ½-inch watermelon cubes (see Note)

4½ tablespoons light corn syrup

1 thin sliver fresh ginger root (optional)

2½ teaspoons fresh lemon juice

⅓ cup plus 1 tablespoon frozen cranberry juice cocktail concentrate

Makes generous 1½ pints, 6 servings.

Spread melon cubes on aluminum foil–lined baking sheet. Cover with wax paper. Freeze for 1½ hours or until frozen, and up to 24 hours. (For longer storage, peel cubes from foil and freeze in plastic bag for up to a month.)

Combine corn syrup, ginger root (if used), and lemon juice in a small bowl or cup and stir until well blended. Cover with plastic wrap. Place in freezer for 30 minutes or until very cold. (Let syrup thaw before using if you inadvertently freeze it for too long.)

Place frozen melon cubes in a food processor fitted with a steel blade. In on/off pulses, chop cubes very finely, stopping and scraping down bowl sides with a rubber spatula several times. Then, processing con-

Watermelon Sorbet with Easy Mango Sorbet *(recipe on pages 117–18)* and
Honeydew-Lime Sorbet *(recipe on pages 118–19)*

tinuously, purée mixture for about 1 minute longer. (If mixture is too cold and stiff to process smoothly, stop and scrape down bowl sides frequently or let stand to soften just slightly before continuing.) Remove ginger root from chilled syrup. Add syrup and cranberry juice concentrate to processor, briefly stirring to incorporate. Continue puréeing for about 2 minutes longer, or until sorbet is well blended and *completely smooth.* Stop processor and scrape down sides several times. For smoothest texture do not underprocess.

Sorbet may be served immediately but is a little firmer if transferred to a chilled storage container and placed in freezer for 30 minutes before serving. Store in freezer for up to a week; let soften for a few minutes before serving if too firm.

Note: You will need about 5 pounds of whole watermelon. Use only the most flavorful parts of the flesh and discard the watery portions near the rind. Very brightly colored and intensely flavored melons yield the most appealing sorbet.

Variation: Sorbet-Filled Watermelon Slices

Use the shell of half a small (11- to 12-inch-long) watermelon; half a Fiery Red mini-watermelon is just the right size to hold *2 batches* of sorbet. Scoop out brightly colored, sweet flesh (use it to prepare sorbet or reserve for another purpose). Reserve a few seeds for garnishing finished sorbet-filled melon slices. Invert shell and drain thoroughly. Pat interior dry with paper towels. Cover and refrigerate until thoroughly chilled.

Prepare 2 batches of watermelon sorbet. (Keep first batch frozen while second is prepared.) Spoon sorbet into shell, packing down firmly to form a solid layer and smoothing so sorbet surface is flush with edge of rind. Immediately cover surface with wax paper and transfer filled shell to freezer. Freeze for 1½ hours, or until sorbet is firm and frozen (do not freeze for so long that the shell becomes frozen solid and difficult to cut). Transfer watermelon to a cutting board and cut crosswise into 11 or 12 slices using a large, sharp knife. If desired, press a reserved seed or two into each slice for garnish. Lay slices on a foil-lined baking sheet and immediately return to freezer for a few minutes, until sorbet freezes firm again. Pack slices in large plastic bags and store, frozen, for 3 or 4 days. Serve slices on plates, just like real watermelon.

Per serving (based on 6 ½-cup servings, or 12 servings Sorbet-Filled Watermelon Slices):
Calories: 87 Grams of fat: 0.4 Grams of saturated fat: 0
Mgrams cholesterol: 0 Mgrams sodium: 13
Percentage of calories from fat: 4

pink grapefruit ice

To me, the loveliest fruit sorbets and ices are those that simply concentrate the essential character of the fruit and offer it up in a luxuriously uncomplicated, frosty-smooth form. These desserts are like distillations, tasting clearer, purer, and fruitier than the fruits themselves. ✽ Grapefruit is not one of my favorite fruits, but this is one of my favorite ices. It is pretty served garnished with several white grapefruit segments and a spring of mint. ✽ The recipe can be varied just slightly to produce an equally delicious granité. Directions are provided at the end of the recipe.

3 1/3 cups strained fresh pink grapefruit juice (preferably from Ruby Red or other rose-fleshed grapefruits)

1/4 cup cranberry juice cocktail concentrate

1/2 teaspoon very finely grated grapefruit zest (yellow part of skin)

1 tablespoon fresh lemon juice

Generous 1/2 cup granulated sugar (use scant 2/3 cup for very tart grapefruits)

1 tablespoon light corn syrup

Makes a scant 1 quart, about 7 servings.

Combine grapefruit juice, cranberry juice concentrate, grapefruit zest, and lemon juice in a nonreactive storage container.

Stir together sugar, corn syrup, and 1/3 cup water in a small nonreactive saucepan. Bring just to a boil over medium heat. Cover and gently boil for 1 1/2 minutes. Remove lid and continue boiling, without stirring, for 2 minutes longer. Stir about 1/2 cup grapefruit juice mixture into sugar syrup until completely

blended and smooth. Return grapefruit-syrup mixture to remainder of grapefruit juice mixture and cover with plastic wrap. Place in freezer for 4 hours or until almost completely frozen but not hard. (Let mixture thaw slightly before using if you inadvertently freeze it for too long and it hardens.)

Place mixture in a food processor. In on/off pulses, chop mixture until fine, stopping and scraping down mixture with a rubber spatula several times. Then process continuously until completely smooth, about 2 minutes longer.

Ice can be served immediately but is a little firmer if placed in a chilled storage container and frozen for 30 minutes before serving. Store in freezer for up to 4 days; if very firm, let soften for a few minutes before serving.

Variation: Pink Grapefruit Granité

Prepare sugar syrup and add to grapefruit juice mixture as directed. Pour mixture into a large, shallow, nonreactive container or bowl. Freeze for at least 4 hours, stirring mixture with a fork to break it up and form icy crystals 3 or 4 times during freezing. Serve granité piled into parfait glasses or sherbet dishes.

Per serving (based on 7 servings):
Calories: 133   Grams of fat: 0.2   Grams of saturated fat: 0
Mgrams cholesterol: 0   Mgrams sodium: 4
Percentage of calories from fat: 1

pineapple-buttermilk sherbet

$\mathscr{B}$uttermilk goes particularly well with pineapple, not only lending a nice tang to this easy, fresh-tasting sherbet but also creating the illusion of creaminess. For best flavor and texture, use only the most tender parts of a very ripe, sweet pineapple; pithy pieces from around the core should be discarded or reserved for another use. ∿ While the sherbet can, of course, be served alone, it is especially tempting topped with Quick Raspberry or Blueberry Sauce (pages 135 and 130–31, respectively).

2 ¾ cups (about 1 pound) fresh, very ripe pineapple chunks
¼ cup fresh orange segments, free of all membrane (see Note)
⅓ cup granulated sugar
1 teaspoon fresh lemon juice
⅓ cup very cold buttermilk

Makes 1 generous pint, about 5 servings.

Spread pineapple chunks and orange segments separately on an aluminum foil–lined baking sheet. Cover loosely with wax paper. Freeze until completely frozen, at least 1½ hours and up to 24 hours, if desired. (For longer storage, peel pieces from foil. Freeze, separately, in plastic bags for up to a month.)

In a small saucepan, combine sugar with 3 table-spoons water and stir until well combined. Bring just to a boil over medium heat. Cover and gently boil for 1½ minutes. Remove lid and continue boiling, without stirring, for 1 minute longer. Transfer syrup to a heat-proof cup. Stir in lemon juice. Cover with plastic wrap. Place in freezer for about 1 hour or until very cold and stiffened but not completely frozen. (If syrup freezes too much, thaw slightly before using.)

Place orange segments in a food processor. In on/off pulses, chop very fine, stopping and scraping down bowl sides with a rubber spatula several times. Add pineapple chunks and continue processing for about 1½ minutes longer, until most chunks are finely chopped. (If pineapple is too hard and cold to process, let stand a few minutes to soften.) Scrape down sides.

Processing continuously, add chilled syrup, then buttermilk through feed tube and continue processing until sherbet is well blended and only some very fine bits of pineapple remain.

Serve immediately or, for a firmer sherbet, transfer to a chilled storage container and freeze for at least 45 minutes before serving. Sherbet may be stored, frozen, for up to a week; let soften for a few minutes before serving if too firm.

Note: For membrane-free segments, remove peel and all white pith from orange. Using a sharp paring knife, cut inward on each side of individual segments to detach them from the membranes.

Per serving (based on 5 servings):
Calories: 98   Grams of fat: 0.5   Grams of saturated fat: 0.1
Mgrams cholesterol: 0   Mgrams sodium: 18
Percentage of calories from fat: 4

easy mango sorbet

𝒯his smooth and colorful mango sorbet has a mild, intriguing taste. It is especially appealing spooned over fresh strawberries. Unlike conventionally prepared sorbets, which require an ice-cream maker, this one is whipped up quickly in a food processor.

3 cups (½-inch chunks) fresh, ripe mango (see Note)
3 tablespoons granulated sugar
1 tablespoon fresh lemon juice

Makes 1½ pints, 5 or 6 servings.

Spread mango chunks on an aluminum foil–lined baking sheet. Cover with wax paper. Freeze for 1½ hours, or until completely frozen, and up to 24 hours, if desired. (For longer storage, peel from foil and freeze in a plastic bag for up to a month.)

Stir together sugar and 3 tablespoons water in a small saucepan. Bring just to a boil over medium heat. Cover and gently boil for 1 minute. Remove lid and continue boiling, without stirring, for 1 minute longer. Transfer syrup to a heatproof cup. Stir in lemon juice. Cover with plastic wrap. Place in freezer for 1½ hours, until icy but not frozen. (Let syrup thaw slightly before using if you inadvertently freeze it.)

Place frozen mango chunks in a food processor fitted with a steel blade. In on/off pulses, chop chunks very finely, stopping and scraping down bowl sides with a rubber spatula several times. (If chunks are too hard to chop easily, let them stand to soften for a few minutes, then continue.) Continue puréeing in on/off pulses for about 30 seconds longer. Processing continuously, add chilled syrup through feed tube. Continue puréeing for 2 minutes longer, scraping down bowl several times, until sorbet is well blended and *completely smooth*; for smoothest texture do not underprocess.

Sorbet can be served immediately but is a little firmer if placed in a chilled storage container and frozen for 30 minutes before serving. Store in freezer for up to a week; if necessary, let soften for a few minutes before serving.

Note: Use unblemished, *fully ripe* mangoes; they will give slightly when pressed and are very aromatic.

Per serving (based on 6 servings):
Calories: 91   Grams of fat: 0.3   Grams of saturated fat: 0.1
Mgrams cholesterol: 0   Mgrams sodium: 2
Percentage of calories from fat: 3

cantaloupe (or honeydew-lime) sorbet

*T*his recipe captures the delicate taste of cantaloupe, heightening it slightly but not obscuring it. A scoop of cantaloupe sorbet is a wonderful addition to mild-flavored fruit salads. ∾ The same recipe can also be used to prepare a delicious, more intensely flavored Honeydew-Lime Sorbet; see the variation at the end of the recipe.

3 cups (about 1 pound) ripe (½-inch) cantaloupe cubes
⅓ cup granulated sugar
Pinch of very finely grated lemon zest
1½ tablespoons fresh lemon juice

Makes 1 generous pint, 4 or 5 servings.

Spread cantaloupe cubes on aluminum foil–lined baking sheet. Cover with wax paper. Place in freezer for 1½ hours, or until frozen, and up to 24 hours. (For longer storage, peel cubes from foil; freeze in plastic bag for up to a month.)

In a small saucepan, combine sugar with ¼ cup water and stir to combine. Bring just to a boil over medium heat. Cover and gently boil for 1½ minutes. Remove lid and continue boiling, without stirring, for 1 minute longer. Transfer syrup to a heatproof cup. Stir in lemon zest and juice. Cover with plastic wrap. Place in freezer for 1 hour, or until very cold and stiffened but not completely frozen. (Let syrup thaw slightly before using if you inadvertently freeze it too long.)

Place frozen melon cubes in a food processor fitted with a steel blade. In on/off pulses, chop cubes very finely, stopping and scraping down bowl sides with a rubber spatula several times. Then, processing continuously, purée mixture for about 1½ minutes longer, until very smooth. Scrape down sides. (If pieces are too cold and hard to process easily, set aside to soften slightly before continuing.) Processing continuously, add chilled syrup through feed tube and continue puréeing for about 2 minutes longer, until sorbet is well blended and *completely smooth;* for smoothest texture do not underprocess.

Sorbet may be served immediately but is a little firmer if transferred to a chilled storage container and placed in freezer for 30 minutes before serving. Store in freezer for up to a week; let soften for a few minutes before serving if too firm.

Variation: Honeydew-Lime Sorbet

Prepare exactly as for cantaloupe sorbet, except use 3 cups honeydew melon cubes, 1 generous pinch lime zest, and 1½ tablespoons lime juice in place of the cantaloupe and lemon zest and juice.

Per serving (Cantaloupe—5 servings):
Calories: 83   Grams of fat: 0.3   Grams of saturated fat: 0
Mgrams cholesterol: 0   Mgrams sodium: 8
Percentage of calories from fat: 3

Per serving (Honeydew-Lime—5 servings):
Calories: 85   Grams of fat: 0.1   Grams of saturated fat: 0
Mgrams cholesterol: 0   Mgrams sodium: 10
Percentage of calories from fat: 1

easy raspberry ice

*F*resh raspberries are often hard to find, and they are always pricey, so I've come to rely on thawed frozen berries in syrup to make this tempting, easy-to-prepare ice. Since most companies process and freeze the raspberries while still very fresh, they usually have a bright color and flavor. Moreover, because the berries are packed in syrup, they need only to be sieved and combined with a little lemon juice, corn syrup, and water and they are ready to use.

2 (10-ounce) packages frozen red raspberries in syrup, thawed
1 tablespoon plus 2 teaspoons fresh lemon juice
3 tablespoons light corn syrup
1 tablespoon raspberry liqueur (optional)

Makes scant 1 quart, 8 servings.

Press raspberries through a fine sieve into a medium-sized nonreactive bowl. Stir in lemon juice, corn syrup, liqueur (if used), and 1 cup water, until evenly incorporated.

Cover and freeze mixture for at least 4 hours, or until mixture is frozen and firm but not completely hard. (Let mixture thaw slightly before using if you inadvertently freeze it for too long.)

Place frozen mixture in a food processor. (Return storage container to freezer so that it stays cold while you process ice mixture.) In on/off pulses, process

Lemon Ice with Honeydew-Lime Sorbet *(recipe on pages 118–19)*

mixture until fine, stopping and scraping down mixture with a rubber spatula several times. Then process continuously until completely smooth, about 1½ minutes longer. Return ice to chilled container and freeze for at least 45 minutes or until firm before serving. (It will become even firmer upon longer storage.)

Store in freezer for up to 3 days; if very firm let soften for a few minutes before serving.

Per serving (based on 8 servings):
Calories: 116   Grams of fat: 0.1   Grams of saturated fat: 0.1
Mgrams cholesterol: 0   Mgrams sodium: 7
Percentage of calories from fat: 1

Lemon Ice

𝒜 scoop or two of Lemon Ice mounded in a sherbet dish and accented with a sprig of lemon balm or mint is a most welcome dessert on sticky, hot days. The taste is clean and clear and just puckery enough to revive flagging spirits and summer-dulled appetites.

¾ cup fresh lemon juice

¼ cup fresh orange juice

2 teaspoons very finely grated lemon zest (yellow part of skin)

½ cup plus 2 tablespoons granulated sugar

¼ cup light corn syrup

Makes a generous 1½ pints, 6 or 7 servings.

Combine lemon juice, orange juice, and lemon zest in a medium-sized nonreactive storage container.

Stir together sugar, corn syrup, and ⅓ cup water in a small saucepan. Bring just to a boil over medium heat. Cover and gently boil for 1½ minutes. Remove lid and continue boiling, without stirring, for 2 minutes longer. Stir 1½ cups water into sugar syrup, until completely blended and smooth. Then stir sugar syrup into lemon juice mixture. Cover with plastic wrap. Refrigerate for at least 1 hour and up to 4 hours, if

desired. Strain mixture through a fine sieve. Return to container and freeze for 4½ hours or until frozen but not completely hard. (Let mixture thaw slightly before using if you inadvertently freeze it for too long.)

Place mixture in a food processor. (Return storage container to freezer so that it stays cold while you process the ice mixture.) In on/off pulses, chop mixture until fine, stopping and scraping down mixture with a rubber spatula several times. Then process continuously until *completely smooth*, about 2 minutes longer. Return ice to chilled container and freeze for at least 45 minutes or until firm before serving. (It will become even firmer upon longer storage.)

Store in freezer for up to 3 days; if very firm let soften for a few minutes before serving.

Per serving (based on 7 servings):
Calories: 109   Grams of fat: 0   Grams of saturated fat: 0
Mgrams cholesterol: 0   Mgrams sodium: 9
Percentage of calories from fat: 0

minted lime ice

$\mathcal{T}$here is a wonderful pungency and edge to fresh lime that simultaneously clears the palate and the head. Add a touch of cool, invigorating crème de menthe, serve the combination frozen, and the result is one of the most bracing of treats. It makes a fine between-courses refresher or a simple hot weather dessert. ∾ For a completely different, richer dessert presentation, try serving scoops of the emerald-colored ice drizzled with Minted Chocolate Sauce (a variation on page 133) and garnished with a few shards of bittersweet chocolate. The exotic combination of mint, citrus, and smooth and crisp chocolate is unexpected and visually and texturally interesting, not to mention quite good (see Note at the end of the recipe). ∾ This recipe can be made with or without fresh peppermint leaves. (Vary the amount depending on the pepperiness of the leaves; do not substitute other mint varieties.) Prepare the mintier version if you plan to serve the ice with chocolate.

⅔ cup fresh lime juice

1½ teaspoons very finely grated lime zest (green part of skin)

⅓ to ½ cup coarsely chopped fresh peppermint leaves (optional)

⅔ cup granulated sugar

¼ cup light corn syrup

3 tablespoons green crème de menthe

Makes a generous 1½ pints, 6 or 7 servings.

Combine lime juice and zest and peppermint leaves (if used) in a medium-sized nonreactive storage container.

Stir together sugar, corn syrup, crème de menthe, and ⅓ cup water in a small saucepan. Bring just to a boil over medium heat. Cover and gently boil for 1½ minutes. Remove lid and continue boiling, without stirring, for 2 minutes longer. Stir 1¾ cups water into sugar syrup, until completely blended and smooth. Then stir sugar syrup into lime juice mixture. Cover with plastic wrap. Refrigerate for at least 1 hour and up to 4 hours, if desired. Strain mixture through a fine sieve. Return to container and freeze for 4½ hours, or until frozen but not completely hard. (Let mixture thaw slightly before using if you inadvertently freeze it for too long.)

Place mixture in a food processor. (Return storage container to freezer so it will stay cold while you process the ice mixture.) In on/off pulses, chop mixture until fine, stopping and scraping down mixture with a rubber spatula several times. Then process continuously until completely smooth, about 2 minutes longer. Return ice to chilled container and freeze for at least

45 minutes before serving. (It will become slightly firmer upon longer storage.

Store in freezer for up to 3 days.

Note: If serving ice with chocolate, prepare 1 recipe Minted Chocolate Sauce (page 133) and chill thoroughly. Grate ½ ounce bittersweet (not unsweetened) chocolate into shards. Top ice with sauce and grated chocolate just before serving.

Per serving (based on 7 servings):
Calories: 109   Grams of fat: 0   Grams of saturated fat: 0
Mgrams cholesterol: 0   Mgrams sodium: 9
Percentage of calories from fat: 0

Per serving (with Minted Chocolate Sauce and chocolate shards):
Calories: 352   Grams of fat: 4.6   Grams of saturated fat: 0.4
Mgrams cholesterol: 1   Mgrams sodium: 37
Percentage of calories from fat: 11

two-color frozen dessert ring filled with fruit

*T*his colorful dessert ring features one layer each of Easy Raspberry Ice and Peach (or Peach-Strawberry) Light Ice Cream surrounding liqueur-spiked melon balls and berries. It looks festive and makes an easy, light, and refreshing party dessert.

1 recipe Easy Raspberry Ice (pages 119–21)
1 recipe Peach Light Ice Cream *or* Peach-Strawberry Light
    Ice Cream (page 124)
1½ to 2 cups mixed honeydew and cantaloupe balls
½ tablespoon kirsch (cherry brandy)
1 tablespoon granulated sugar
¾ to 1 cup mixed fresh strawberries, blueberries,
    and raspberries

Makes 9 to 12 servings.

Set an 8-cup or similar-size decorative ring mold in freezer until well chilled. Press raspberry ice firmly into mold to form a smooth layer. Return to freezer to firm up ice before continuing, if necessary. Repeat process with ice cream, pressing firmly into place.

Cover and return to freezer for at least 2 hours and up to 24 hours, if preferred.

Shortly before serving time, stir together melon balls, kirsch, and sugar until well blended. Chill for at least 30 minutes. Chill berries in a separate container.

At serving time, dip mold in warm water for about 5 to 7 seconds (don't overdo it). Invert and shake to release ring onto serving plate. Immediately return to freezer briefly to firm up surface. Stir berries into melon mixture. Spoon fruit into center of mold and serve immediately. Cut dessert into servings with a large knife.

Per serving (based on 12 servings):
Calories: 171   Grams of fat: 2.0   Grams of saturated fat: 1.1
Mgrams cholesterol: 7   Mgrams sodium: 46
Percentage of calories from fat: 10

Peach light ice cream

$\mathscr{P}$eaches and cream is one of the truly ambrosial flavor combinations, and in this very light, very peachy ice cream it comes through clearly. In fact, it's amazing just how lush this ice cream is considering the modest amount of cream it contains. ∿ The same basic recipe can also be used to prepare an equally delectable peach-strawberry light ice cream; see the variation at the end of recipe.

3 cups (about 1 pound) fresh peach slices tossed with
   1½ tablespoons fresh lemon juice
¼ cup chilled heavy (whipping) cream
1 recipe Improved Italian Meringue (pages 150–51),
   see Note

Makes generous 1 quart, 8 servings.

Spread peaches and lemon juice on aluminum foil–lined baking sheet. Cover with wax paper. Place in freezer for about 1 hour, or until frozen but not completely hard. (If you inadvertently freeze peaches for too long and they become too hard, let thaw slightly before using.)

Place peach slices in a food processor fitted with a steel blade. In on/off pulses, chop slices finely, stopping and scraping down bowl sides with a rubber spatula several times. Add cream and continue puréeing in on/off pulses for about 1 minute longer. If mixture is too stiff, let stand for about 5 minutes to soften slightly. Then purée until mixture is well blended and fairly smooth, stopping and scraping down bowl frequently; some small bits of peach may remain.

Using a wire whisk, whisk peach mixture into partially frozen meringue, until mixture is smoothly incorporated. Immediately turn out ice cream into storage container. Freeze for at least 2 hours and up to 48 hours in very cold freezer; ice cream will not freeze hard.

Note: Prepare Italian meringue as directed, except immediately place in freezer until partially frozen and slightly stiff, about 1 hour.

Variation: Peach-Strawberry Light Ice Cream
Use 2 cups peach slices and toss with 2 teaspoons lemon juice. Spread on baking sheet. Sprinkle 1 cup coarsely sliced fresh strawberries over peaches. Proceed as directed.

Per serving (Peach—based on 8 servings):
Calories: 137   Grams of fat: 2.8   Grams of saturated fat: 1.7
Mgrams cholesterol: 10   Mgrams sodium: 59
Percentage of calories from fat: 18

Per serving (Peach-Strawberry—based on 8 servings):
Calories: 133   Grams of fat: 2.9   Grams of saturated fat: 1.7
Mgrams cholesterol: 10   Mgrams sodium: 59
Percentage of calories from fat: 18

SAUCES, FROSTINGS, AND FINISHING TOUCHES

Lemon Cake Roll with Lemon Cream *(recipe on pages 21–22)* and Blackberry Sauce

blackberry sauce

*I*ntense and complex in flavor and brilliantly colored, this sauce is a matchless accompaniment to bold, zesty desserts featuring lemon, orange or lime. It is especially good pooled around Lemon Chiffon Mousse (pages 88–89) or drizzled over Lemon Ice (page 121) or Peach Light Ice Cream (page 124).

2 ⅔ cups fresh or unsweetened frozen blackberries

¼ to ⅓ cup granulated sugar (use larger amount if berries are very tart)

2 teaspoons fresh lemon juice

2 ½ teaspoons cornstarch

Generous pinch of lemon zest (yellow part of skin)

Makes 1¼ cups, or 8 (2½-tablespoon) servings.

In a medium-sized saucepan, stir together berries and sugar. Bring to a simmer over medium heat, stirring until sugar dissolves. Continue simmering for about 2 minutes, until berries begin to release juice. In a small bowl or cup, stir together lemon juice, 1 tablespoon cold water, and the cornstarch, until well blended. Stir cornstarch mixture and lemon zest into berry mixture and continue simmering until mixture thickens and clears, about 2 minutes longer. Press mixture through a fine sieve, forcing through as much juice and pulp as possible and discarding seeds.

Refrigerate sauce in a nonreactive storage container for at least 1 hour, or until chilled, before serving. Sauce keeps, refrigerated, for 3 or 4 days. Stir briefly before using. If sauce seems too thick, thin it with a little orange juice or water before serving.

Per serving (based on 8 servings):
Calories: 50   Grams of fat: 0.2   Grams of saturated fat: 0
Mgrams cholesterol: 0   Mgrams sodium: 0
Percentage of calories from fat: 3

fluffy white frosting

A simple amalgam of beaten egg whites and sugar, this billowy, marshmallow-like meringue frosting is completely fat-free. ∿ A problem with many old-fashioned versions of meringue frostings is that they call for merely warming the whites in the top of a double boiler, rather than heating them to 160° F. as current food-handling practices dictate. My updated recipe, however, has been carefully devised to ensure safety. Though it is similar to the classic recipe for Italian meringue—boiling sugar syrup is added as egg whites are beaten—there are several important differences: The whites are warmed to almost hot before being beaten; the sugar syrup is heated to a higher temperature than usual; and the syrup is added so rapidly that the whites are actually cooked by its heat.

2 large egg whites, completely free of yolk

1½ tablespoons light corn syrup

⅔ cup minus 1 tablespoon granulated sugar

Generous pinch of salt

¾ teaspoon vanilla extract

Makes about 12 servings, enough frosting to cover a 2- or 3-layer 8½-inch cake or a 13- by 7½-inch sheet cake.

Place whites in a large grease-free mixer bowl. Set the bowl of whites in a larger bowl of very hot tap water and let stand for 10 minutes, stirring occasionally. Combine corn syrup, ¼ cup water, and the sugar in a 2-quart saucepan, stirring until well blended. Bring to a simmer over medium-high heat. Cover and boil for 2 minutes to allow steam to wash any sugar from pan sides. Uncover and continue simmering, *without stirring,* for about 2 minutes longer, or until mixture bubbles loudly and reaches 244° F. to

245° F. on a candy thermometer. (To test for doneness without a candy thermometer, drop a teaspoon of syrup into ice water; when cooked to the correct temperature syrup will form a firm but not quite brittle ball that holds its shape when squeezed.) Immediately remove pan from heat and set aside.

Transfer mixer bowl to mixer and beat whites on medium speed until very frothy and opaque. Raise speed to high and beat until whites just begin to stand in soft peaks; be careful not to overbeat. Meanwhile, return syrup to burner and reheat just to boiling. Beating whites on high speed, *immediately* begin pouring boiling syrup in a stream *down bowl sides* (avoid beaters or syrup will stick to them or be thrown onto bowl sides), pouring rapidly enough that all syrup is incorporated in about 15 seconds. Add salt and continue beating on high speed until mixture is stiffened, glossy, and cooled to barely warm. Beat in vanilla until evenly incorporated.

Frost cake immediately, swirling frosting decoratively with a table knife or back of a spoon, or store frosting airtight for up to 48 hours; frosting may soften and gradually deflate upon longer standing.

Variation: Fluffy Seafoam Frosting

Prepare exactly as for Fluffy White Frosting, except substitute scant ⅔ cup packed light brown sugar for the granulated sugar.

Variation: Fluffy Orange Seafoam Frosting

Prepare exactly as for Fluffy White Frosting except substitute scant ⅔ cup packed light brown sugar for the granulated sugar and add scant ½ teaspoon very finely grated orange zest (orange part of peel) along with vanilla.

Per serving (based on 12 servings):
Calories: 51   Grams of fat: 0   Grams of saturated fat: 0
Mgrams cholesterol: 0   Mgrams sodium: 33
Percentage of calories from fat: 0

fluffy chocolate frosting

*L*ike the Fluffy White Frosting on pages 128–29, this one is designed to satisfy current food-safety guidelines on cooking with eggs. As such, it includes steps to ensure that the egg whites are actually cooked while they are being whipped. Be sure to follow all directions carefully. ⌒ With a taste and texture reminiscent of gooey-soft, chocolate marshmallows, this frosting makes a tempting (but very low-fat) addition to the Chocolate Triple Layer Cake (page 19.)

3 large egg whites, completely free of yolk

½ ounce unsweetened chocolate, coarsely chopped

2½ tablespoons light corn syrup

¾ cup granulated sugar

Generous pinch of salt

¾ teaspoon vanilla extract

¼ teaspoon instant coffee powder or granules dissolved in
    1 teaspoon hot water

¼ cup powdered sugar

3 tablespoons unsweetened cocoa powder

Makes enough frosting to generously cover a 2- or 3-layer 8- or 8½-inch cake; a 13- by 7½-inch sheet cake; or a 10-inch Bundt-style cake.

Place whites in a large grease-free mixer bowl. Set the bowl of whites in a larger bowl of very hot tap water and let stand for 10 minutes, stirring occasionally. In a small heavy saucepan set over lowest heat, melt chocolate, stirring constantly, until smooth; be very careful not to scorch. Set aside to cool slightly.

Combine corn syrup, ¼ cup water and the sugar in a 2-quart saucepan, stirring until well blended. Bring to a simmer over medium-high heat. Cover and boil for 2 minutes to allow steam to wash any sugar from pan sides. Uncover and continue simmering, *without stirring,* for 1½ minutes longer, or until mixture bubbles loudly and reaches 244° F. to 245° F. on a candy thermometer. (To test for doneness without a candy thermometer, drop a teaspoon of syrup into ice water; when cooked to the proper temperature syrup will form a firm ball that holds its shape when squeezed.) Immediately remove pan from heat and set aside.

Transfer mixer bowl to mixer set on medium speed and beat whites until very frothy and opaque. Raise speed to high and beat until whites just begin to stand in soft peaks; be careful not to overbeat. Meanwhile, return syrup to burner and reheat just to boiling. Beating whites on high speed, *immediately* begin pouring boiling syrup in a stream *down bowl sides* (avoid beaters or syrup will stick to them or be thrown onto bowl sides), pouring rapidly enough that all the syrup is incorporated in about 15 seconds. Add salt and continue beating on high speed until mixture is stiffened, glossy, and cooled to barely warm. Beat in vanilla and coffee mixture until evenly incorporated. Sift powdered sugar and cocoa onto a sheet of wax paper. A bit at a time, whisk into egg white mixture. Whisk in chocolate just until smoothly incorporated.

Frost cake immediately, swirling frosting decoratively, or store frosting airtight for up to 48 hours; frosting may soften and gradually deflate upon longer standing.

Per serving (based on 12 servings):
Calories: 79   Grams of fat: 0.8   Grams of saturated fat: 0
Mgrams cholesterol: 0   Mgrams sodium: 39
Percentage of calories from fat: 8

*B*lueberry Sauce makes an appealing, nearly fat-free accompaniment to Deli-Style Lemon Cheesecake (pages 54–56). For a light, colorful summer dessert, serve the sauce over scoops of Pineapple-Buttermilk Sherbet (pages 116–17).

¼ cup granulated sugar, or a little more if berries are
   very tart
1 tablespoon cornstarch
Pinch of ground cinnamon
2½ cups fresh or partially thawed unsweetened
   frozen blueberries
1 tablespoon fresh lemon juice

Generous pinch very finely grated lemon zest (yellow
   part of skin)

Makes about 2 cups or 8 (¼-cup) servings.

In a medium saucepan, stir together sugar, cornstarch, and cinnamon until thoroughly blended. Stir in 1 tablespoon water and the blueberries until incorporated. Bring to a simmer over medium heat, stirring until sugar dissolves and berries begin releasing juice. Continue simmering, stirring occasionally, for 2 to 3 minutes, or until pan liquid thickens slightly and turns clear. Remove from heat. Stir in lemon juice and zest.

Refrigerate sauce in a nonreactive storage container for at least 1 hour, or until chilled, before serving. Sauce keeps, refrigerated, for up to a week. Stir briefly before using.

Per serving (based on 8 servings):
Calories: 51   Grams of fat: 0.2   Grams of saturated fat: 0
Mgrams cholesterol: 0   Mgrams sodium: 3
Percentage of calories from fat: 3

apricot sauce

$\mathcal{S}$un-colored and vibrant, this sweet-tart sauce gets its deep, fruity flavor and aroma from the combination of dried apricots and fresh apricots poached with a bit of citrus. If you can find them, use American apricots; they are brighter in color and taste than most imported varieties. ◆ Apricot sauce is used in both Molded Rum Cream Puddings (pages 82–83) and Apricot Tipsy Parson (pages 93–94).

1 cup orange juice, plus a little extra if needed to thin sauce

⅔ cup finely chopped dried apricots, preferably American

¼ cup granulated sugar

¼ teaspoon grated orange zest (orange part of skin)

⅛ teaspoon grated lemon zest (yellow part of skin)

1½ tablespoons Grand Marnier (or substitute water, if preferred)

4 poached apricots, pitted and drained (or 4 canned apricots in light syrup, pitted and drained)

Makes about 1⅓ cups or 8 (generous 2½-tablespoon) servings.

In a medium saucepan combine 1 cup orange juice, the dried apricots, sugar, and orange and lemon zests. Bring to a simmer over medium heat. Continue simmering, stirring occasionally, for 15 to 20 minutes longer, until all but about ¼ cup juice is absorbed and apricots are very tender. Transfer mixture to a food processor. Add Grand Marnier and poached apricots. Process for 3 to 4 minutes, or until completely smooth. If mixture is thicker than desired, add a bit more orange juice and process to blend. Add juice until desired consistency is obtained.

Turn out sauce into a nonreactive storage container. Refrigerate for at least 1 hour and for up to a week, if desired.

Per serving (based on 8 servings):
Calories: 77   Grams of fat: 0.2   Grams of saturated fat: 0
Mgrams cholesterol: 0   Mgrams sodium: 2
Percentage of calories from fat: 2

glossy bittersweet glaze

*T*his lustrous dark chocolate glaze is used to top the Fudge Bundt Cake (pages 34–35) and also makes a nice addition to the Vanilla Pound Cake (pages 28–29). Though it tastes rich and chocolatey, only 9 percent of its calories come from fat. ∽ As with many of the chocolate recipes in *Dream Desserts*, the success of this one depends on carefully blending cocoa powder and chocolate. Cocoa powder—the product that remains when most of the fat has been pressed from unsweetened chocolate—is used to provide much of the chocolate flavor and color. A bit of unsweetened chocolate—which still contains its natural abundance of fat, or cocoa butter—is added to lend smoothness and round out the cocoa taste.

½ **cup granulated sugar**

3 ½ **tablespoons unsweetened American-style cocoa powder, such as Hershey's**

¼ **teaspoon instant coffee powder or granules**

3 **tablespoons dark corn syrup**

½ **ounce unsweetened chocolate, chopped into ¼-inch pieces**

½ **tablespoon cognac or brandy (or substitute orange juice, if preferred)**

1 **teaspoon vanilla extract**

⅔ **cup sifted powdered sugar**

Makes enough glaze to cover one 9- or 10-inch Bundt cake or pound cake, about 12 servings.

In a medium-sized saucepan, stir together sugar, cocoa, and coffee powder, until completely blended and smooth. Stir in 2 tablespoons hot water and corn syrup, until smoothly incorporated. Bring mixture just to a boil, stirring, over medium-high heat. Boil, stirring, for 2 minutes; remove from heat. Immediately add chocolate, stirring until completely melted and smooth. Stir in cognac, vanilla, and powdered sugar until mixture is completely smooth. Set glaze aside until cooled and thickened slightly, 20 to 30 minutes. (Or, to speed up cooling, refrigerate glaze for a few minutes.)

To glaze cake: Place cooled cake on a wire rack over a sheet of wax paper. Slowly pour glaze over top, drizzling back and forth to create a decorative look. Let cake stand for about 15 minutes, until excess glaze has dripped from sides. Working carefully and using 2 wide spatulas, lift cake from rack to serving plate. Serve immediately or store, covered and in a cool place (but not in the refrigerator), for a day or two.

Per serving (based on 12 servings):
Calories: 75   Grams of fat: 0.8   Grams of saturated fat: 0
Mgrams cholesterol: 0   Mgrams sodium: 4
Percentage of calories from fat: 9

SAUCES, FROSTINGS, AND FINISHING TOUCHES

This dark, glossy, all-purpose sauce is slightly bittersweet and very chocolatey. A combination of unsweetened chocolate and cocoa powder gives it robust flavor without too much fat. It is easy to make and keeps very well. Though it thickens a bit during storage, it is fluid enough to serve straight from the refrigerator if you wish. ∾ The recipe can be modified just slightly to create an appealing Minted Chocolate Sauce; see the variation at the end of recipe.

1½ ounces unsweetened chocolate, chopped into
    ¼-inch pieces
2 tablespoons plus 2 teaspoons unsweetened cocoa powder,
    preferably American-style, such as Hershey's
3 tablespoons packed light brown sugar
¾ teaspoon instant coffee powder or granules
¾ cup light corn syrup
1 tablespoon cognac (optional)
1 teaspoon Browned Butter (page 147) or unsalted butter
2 teaspoons vanilla extract

Makes 1¼ cups, 8 (2½-tablespoon) servings.

Chop chocolate in a food processor or blender until very finely chopped. (If a blender is used, it may be necessary to stop motor and stir to redistribute contents once or twice.)

In a heavy, medium-sized saucepan, stir together cocoa powder, sugar, and coffee, until well combined. Slowly stir in corn syrup, then ¼ cup hot water and the cognac (if used), until very smooth and well blended. Bring mixture to a boil over medium heat, stirring. Boil, stirring and scraping pan bottom, for 1 minute. Immediately remove from heat and stir in butter until melted. Transfer mixture to a food processor or blender. Add vanilla. Process or blend for about 1 minute, until mixture is completely smooth. Serve immediately or transfer to a storage container and keep, refrigerated, for up to 3 weeks. Serve chilled or at room temperature, or rewarm over very low heat until barely warm, if desired.

Variation: Minted Chocolate Sauce

Omit cognac from recipe. Reduce hot water from ¼ cup to 2 tablespoons and add 3 tablespoons white or green crème de menthe along with the water. Proceed exactly as directed.

Per serving (based on 8 servings):
Calories: 156   Grams of fat: 3.6   Grams of saturated fat: 0.3
Mgrams cholesterol: 1   Mgrams sodium: 23
Percentage of calories from fat: 20

Per serving (Minted Chocolate Sauce—based on 8 servings):
Calories: 180   Grams of fat: 3.6   Grams of saturated fat: 0.3
Mgrams cholesterol: 1   Mgrams sodium: 23
Percentage of calories from fat: 17

caramel sauce

Although caramel sauce is usually made by boiling water and sugar to the caramel stage, I find that melting and caramelizing the sugar and a little corn syrup produces a much mellower and more sumptuous flavor. It also lends the sauce a distinctive tawny color that ordinary versions lack. But, perhaps the greatest advantage of this alternate method is that the caramel is so rich-tasting that the sauce requires considerably less butterfat than most other caramel sauces. This is far more luxurious and full-bodied than its nutritional analysis suggests. ⁓ For safety reasons and to ensure good results, it is important to prepare this recipe exactly as directed. Take particular care to avoid being burned by splattering or steam when the cream is added to the caramelized sugar. And to eliminate the chance of curdling the sauce, be sure that the caramel mixture has cooled to warm before adding it to the milk.

3 tablespoons heavy (whipping) cream

¾ cup granulated sugar

2½ tablespoons light corn syrup

⅓ cup skim milk

Pinch of salt

1 teaspoon vanilla extract

Makes a scant 1 cup or 8 (2-tablespoon) servings.

In a medium-sized heavy saucepan set over medium-high heat, bring cream and 3 tablespoons water to a simmer. Set aside. In another medium-sized saucepan set over high heat, combine sugar and corn syrup. Heat, stirring constantly, until sugar melts and mixture turns a rich golden brown, about 5 minutes. Immediately remove from heat. *Working with a long-handled wooden spoon and being very careful to avoid splattering,* stir hot cream mixture into sugar mixture. Continue stirring until splattering subsides, the hot cream is incorporated into sugar, and the mixture turns a rich, tawny caramel color. As soon as this color is reached, stir in 2½ tablespoons cold water to stop the cooking process. Set aside until mixture is cooled to warm, about 15 minutes. Meanwhile, in saucepan used to heat cream, heat milk and salt over medium heat until milk just comes to a simmer. Remove from heat and stir in vanilla.

When caramel mixture is *cooled to warm,* gradually stir it into milk mixture. Strain sauce through a fine sieve into a storage container. Serve sauce barely warm, at room temperature, or chilled, depending on what it is accompanying.

Sauce keeps, refrigerated, for up to a week. If serving warm, reheat over medium heat, stirring frequently. Stir well before serving.

Per serving (based on 8 servings):
Calories: 104   Grams of fat: 2.0   Grams of saturated fat: 1.2
Mgrams cholesterol: 8   Mgrams sodium: 46
Percentage of calories from fat: 18

quick raspberry sauce

*R*aspberry sauce is such an appealing accent for so many desserts, I don't like having to depend on the uncertain supply of fresh raspberries to prepare it. Frozen berries, which are almost always available in the markets and can be conveniently stocked in the home freezer, make a very satisfactory sauce on only a few moments' notice. (Packages can be partially defrosted in hot water; then the berries can be removed and thawed in a microwave oven.) ～ The small amount of cornstarch in this sauce does not actually thicken it, but adds body to it so that it flows and covers a plate more attractively.

1 (10-ounce) package frozen red raspberries in syrup, thawed

1 teaspoon cornstarch

Makes about ¼ cup or 6 (2-tablespoon) servings.

Press berries through a fine sieve into a small saucepan; force through as much pulp and syrup as possible and discard seeds. Scrape any pulp clinging to underside of sieve into pan. Transfer 2 tablespoons sieved mixture to a small bowl or cup and add cornstarch; stir until blended. Return cornstarch mixture to saucepan. Bring mixture to a simmer over medium-high heat. Simmer, stirring, for about 1 minute, until sauce becomes just slightly thickened and clear. Remove from heat.

Refrigerate sauce in a nonreactive storage container for at least 30 minutes, or until chilled, before serving. Sauce keeps, refrigerated, for 3 or 4 days. Stir briefly before using.

Per serving (based on 6 servings):
Calories: 50   Grams of fat: 0.1   Grams of saturated fat: 0
Mgrams cholesterol: 0   Mgrams sodium: 0
Percentage of calories from fat: 1

candied citrus zest shreds

Candied shreds of citrus zest are a wonderful, fat-free way to add bright color, welcome texture, and a burst of flavor to desserts. I often use them to add zip to fruit salads and fresh fruit and sorbet cups. They also add appealing textural contrast to mousses, custards, and other very smooth desserts. ∼ Any of the citrus zests suggested here can be candied with good results. Each, of course, lends its own distinctive aroma and taste. Candied orange shreds are nice sprinkled over mixed citrus slices or Lemon Ice (page 121), or as a garnish for the Caramel-Glazed Ginger Custards (pages 80–81). Try the lemon shreds over the Lemon Chiffon Mousse (pages 88–89). ∼ With a minor modification (see the variation at the end of the recipe), ginger root can be candied and used just like citrus shreds. It goes beautifully with fresh orange slices.

½ cup fresh, very thin matchstick-length strips lemon,
   lime, orange, or grapefruit zest (colored part of skin),
   completely free of any white pith
⅓ cup granulated sugar
1 tablespoon light corn syrup

Makes ½ cup candied shreds, enough to garnish
10 to 12 dessert servings.

In a medium-sized saucepan set over medium-high heat, combine zest strips and 1 cup water. Bring to a boil and cook for 3 minutes. Turn out zest into a sieve. Rinse zest under cool water; let drain.

Rinse out saucepan. Add sugar, corn syrup, and 2½ tablespoons water to the rinsed saucepan and stir until well blended. Bring mixture to a simmer over medium-high heat. Cover and simmer for 2 minutes to wash any sugar from pan sides. Using a clean spoon, stir drained zest strips into sugar syrup. Bring mixture to a simmer over medium-high heat. Adjust heat so mixture simmers gently and cook, stirring occasionally, for about 3 to 4 minutes, or just until shreds of zest are tender and translucent. Remove shreds with tines of a fork, spreading them out on a sheet of wax paper until thoroughly cooled. (If desired, reserve the syrup for drizzling over an appropriate fresh or poached fruit dish.)

Candied shreds may be used immediately or wrapped in a clean sheet of wax paper and then placed in an airtight bag or jar. They will keep, refrigerated, for up to 10 days and frozen for a month. Let come to room temperature before using. Separate with the tines of a fork.

SAUCES, FROSTINGS, AND FINISHING TOUCHES

Variation: Candied Fresh Ginger Shreds

Substitute ½ cup peeled matchstick-length strips fresh, peeled ginger root for citrus shreds. Omit blanching of ginger shreds. Combine sugar, corn syrup, and water and bring to a simmer, covered, as

directed. Uncover, add ginger shreds, and proceed as directed.

Per serving (based on 12 servings):
Calories: 12   Grams of fat: 0   Grams of saturated fat: 0
Mgrams cholesterol: 0   Mgrams sodium: 0
Percentage of calories from fat: 0

lemon sauce (or filling)

This easy sauce is intensely lemony, both in color and flavor. Its zestiness, citrusy aroma, and fresh, bold taste make it a particularly nice accompaniment to gingerbread and other very spicy, molasses-scented desserts. ◦ The basic preparation can be modified just slightly (see the variation at the end of the recipe) to yield a fine lemon filling.

2 tablespoons cornstarch

⅔ cup granulated sugar

1 large egg yolk

¼ cup fresh lemon juice

½ tablespoon grated lemon zest (yellow part of skin)

6 tablespoons fresh orange juice

½ teaspoon vanilla extract

1 teaspoon unsalted butter (optional)

Makes 1 cup sauce or 8 (2-tablespoon) servings.

In a medium-sized saucepan, stir together cornstarch and sugar until completely blended and smooth. Stir in egg yolk and lemon juice and zest, until smoothly incorporated. Add orange juice and a generous ½ cup hot water. Bring mixture to a simmer over medium heat, stirring. Cook, stirring, just until mixture

thickens and boils for 1½ minutes; remove from heat. Stir in vanilla and butter (if used), until butter melts. Strain through a sieve into a storage container. Chill for at least 45 minutes or until cool and slightly thickened before using. Sauce may be stored in the refrigerator for up to 48 hours. Stir well before using.

Variation: Lemon Filling

Increase cornstarch to 2 tablespoons plus 2 teaspoons. Decrease water to ⅓ cup.

Per serving (based on 8 servings):
Calories: 87   Grams of fat: 1.2   Grams of saturated fat: 0.5
Mgrams cholesterol: 28   Mgrams sodium: 1
Percentage of calories from fat: 11

Per serving (without butter):
Calories: 83   Grams of fat: 0.7   Grams of saturated fat: 0.2
Mgrams cholesterol: 26   Mgrams sodium: 1
Percentage of calories from fat: 7

almond (or pecan) praline

*N*uts are very oily (often 80 to 85 percent of their calories come from fat!) so they can have only a limited place in reduced-fat recipes. But they are such a distinctive and enticing element in dessert-making that it would be a shame to banish them completely. ~ One way to get the most taste and texture out of small quantities of nuts is to toast them (to intensify flavor) and incorporate them into a praline that can then be lightly sprinkled over desserts. When used in this way, a few nuts go a long, long way. ~ The same basic method given here for pecans and almonds can also be used with hazelnuts. However, these take longer to toast and the hulls need to be removed before using. A maple-flavored praline can also be prepared using the basic recipe. Details are provided in the variations at the end of the recipe. ~ Praline can be made ahead and stored for up to several months in the freezer.

3 tablespoons chopped pecans or almonds

⅓ cup granulated sugar

Makes about ½ cup or 8 (1-tablespoon) servings.

Preheat oven to 350° F. Spread nuts in a baking dish. Place in oven and toast, stirring frequently, for 6 to 9 minutes, or until tinged with brown and fragrant; be careful not to burn. Set nuts aside to cool. Line a heatproof platter or plate with aluminum foil. Lightly oil foil.

Combine sugar and 2 tablespoons water in a small, heavy saucepan over medium-high heat. Bring to a boil, swirling mixture several times to dissolve sugar. Cook, covered, for 2 minutes. Uncover and cook for about 2 to 2½ minutes longer, or until syrup thickens slightly, bubbles, and turns deep amber but *not* dark brown. Using a long-handled wooden spoon, immediately stir nuts into syrup, tossing to coat them; be

careful not to splash as mixture is extremely hot. Then quickly turn out praline onto foil. Let mixture stand for about 10 minutes, or until cold. (Or speed up process by lifting foil and partially cooled brittle from plate and refrigerating until well chilled.) Transfer thoroughly cooled brittle to a heavy plastic bag. Crack mixture into tiny pieces using a mallet or back of a heavy spoon. Use praline immediately or store airtight in refrigerator for several weeks or in the freezer for up to 2 months.

Variation: Hazelnut Praline

Use 3 tablespoons hazelnuts. Spread in a baking dish and toast at 350° F. for 14 to 18 minutes, or until hulls are loosened and nuts are tinged with brown. Set aside until cooled. Rub the nuts between your palms or in a kitchen towel, loosening and discarding the hulls as you work. (Nuts do not have to be completely

Maple-Glazed Maple Custards *(recipe on pages 92–95)* with Maple-Pecan Praline

free of hull.) Chop the hazelnuts. Then proceed with remainder of recipe as directed.

Variation: Maple-Pecan Praline
Reduce sugar to 3 1/2 tablespoons and add 2 tablespoons maple syrup. Reduce water to 1 tablespoon. Proceed as directed, except *watch carefully until syrup changes color from pale brown to dark amber.* Immediately remove from heat and stir in nuts; proceed with recipe exactly as directed.

Per serving (based on 8 servings):
Calories: 47   Grams of fat: 1.7   Grams of saturated fat: 0.1
Mgrams cholesterol: 0   Mgrams sodium: 0
Percentage of calories from fat: 31

fruit crème

I devised this vanilla- and liqueur-scented sauce to be used in place of a whipped cream garnish. It is a perfect complement to most fruit desserts as well as fresh peaches, cherries, and all sorts of berries. It can even be served as a light dip for a platter of fruit. ∼ Though rich-tasting, it is far less fatty than whipped cream: One 3-tablespoon serving contains 2 grams of fat compared to more than 8 grams for 3 tablespoons of whipped cream.

1/3 cup plain nonfat yogurt

3 to 4 tablespoons granulated sugar, to taste

1 tablespoon Grand Marnier or kirsch (cherry brandy), or substitute orange juice, if preferred

1 1/4 teaspoons vanilla extract

1 teaspoon fresh lemon juice

1/8 teaspoon finely grated lemon zest (yellow part of skin)

1 cup 1-percent fat, salt-free cottage cheese

2 ounces reduced-fat cream cheese (sometimes called Neufchâtel cheese), cut into chunks

Makes 1 1/2 cups or 8 (3-tablespoon) servings.

Combine yogurt, sugar, Grand Marnier, vanilla, and lemon juice and zest in a blender (see Note). Blend for 30 seconds. Add cottage cheese and blend for 1 minute. Stop motor and carefully scrape down container sides with a rubber spatula. Blend for 30 seconds longer. With motor running, add cream cheese chunks through blender cap. Blend for 30 seconds. Carefully scrape down sides again. Blend for 30 seconds longer.

Cover and refrigerate for at least 1 hour and up to 3 days, if desired. Thin sauce with a teaspoon or two of water if it stiffens during storage. Stir before serving.

Note: If a blender is unavailable a processor may be substituted, but the sauce will not be quite as smooth.

Per serving (based on 8 servings):
Calories: 68   Grams of fat: 2   Grams of saturated fat: 1.2
Mgrams cholesterol: 7   Mgrams sodium: 35
Percentage of calories from fat: 27

SAUCES, FROSTINGS, AND FINISHING TOUCHES

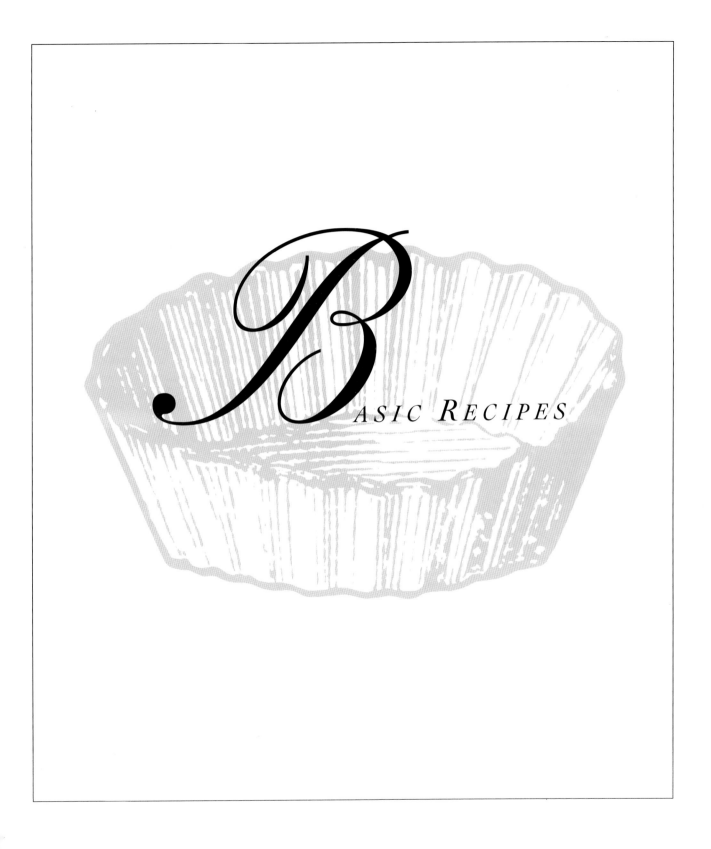

BASIC RECIPES

meringues (or meringue pie shell)

$\mathcal{S}$weet, chewy-crisp and mellow-tasting, meringues were a dessert favorite long before most people ever concerned themselves with nutrition and proper diet. Not only are these treats incredibly low in fat, but they are extremely versatile, serving nicely as individual dessert shells, pie crusts, and airy layers for cakes and tortes. $\backsim$ For a quick, delicious and very low-fat dessert, simply tuck small dollops of low-fat frozen vanilla yogurt or light ice cream into plain meringue shells and top with lightly sugared raspberries or strawberry slices.

½ cup (about 4 large) egg whites, at room temperature and
    completely free of yolk
Generous ¼ teaspoon cream of tartar
¾ cup granulated sugar
⅛ teaspoon salt
1 teaspoon vanilla extract
½ cup powdered sugar

Makes about eight 4½-inch shells or rings;
variation makes 1 pie shell, about 8 servings.

Preheat oven to 225° F. Line two 12- by 15-inch (or similar-size) baking sheets with baking parchment or aluminum foil. If foil is used, grease or spray with nonstick spray coating.

In a large, grease-free mixer bowl with mixer set on low speed, beat egg whites for 30 seconds. Gradu-ally raise speed to high and continue beating until whites are frothy and opaque. Add cream of tartar; continue beating until whites just begin to form soft peaks. Immediately begin adding granulated sugar, about 2 tablespoons at a time, until all is incorporated. Beat in salt and vanilla. Continue to beat until meringue stands in glossy and stiff but not dry peaks, about 1½ minutes longer. Sift powdered sugar over mixture. Using a rubber spatula, fold in until evenly incorporated.

Shape meringues as follows: Using a large pastry bag fitted with a ½-inch diameter plain or open-star tip, pipe mixture into 3½- to 4-inch round meringue shells or thick rings, spacing about 2 inches apart. (A shell should have a solid round base and a ring should be open on the bottom.) Build up sides of shells or rings by tracing the perimeter and piping a second line on top of the first. (Alternatively, form simple meringue rounds by spooning dollops of mixture onto sheet, then hollowing out center of mounds and forming rough rounds using back of a spoon.)

Place pans on separate racks in center half of oven. Bake for 1 hour and switch positions of pans. Bake 1 hour longer or until meringues are firm, dry, and faintly colored. Transfer meringues (with paper still attached) to wire rack and let cool thoroughly. Gently peel off paper. (If paper sticks, meringues are not done. Return to preheated 225°F. oven and bake for 15 to 20 minutes longer.) Carefully pack completely cooled meringues airtight, with no extra headroom in bag or container, until serving time. Meringues may be stored in a cool place for up to a week or they may be wrapped well and frozen for up to a month.

Variation: Meringue Pie Shell

Preheat oven to 250°F. Line a 10-inch pie plate or 9½-inch deep-dish pie plate with aluminum foil, dull side visible; foil should overlap by at least 1 inch all around. Fold foil edges firmly over plate edges to fix it in place. Grease foil or spray with nonstick spray coating.

Prepare meringue mixture exactly as for individual meringues. Turn out mixture into prepared pie plate.

Using back of a spoon, hollow out center and spread mixture up sides to form pie shell.

Bake on center oven rack for 1 hour. Lower heat to 225°F. and bake for 60 to 75 minutes longer, until shell is firm, dry, and faintly tinged with brown. (Shell baked in 9½-inch deep-dish plate may take longer.) Turn off oven and let shell stand in oven for 30 minutes. Transfer pie plate to wire rack and let meringue cool thoroughly. Lift meringue and foil from plate. Gently peel aluminum foil from meringue. (If underside is soft and sticky, meringue is not done. Lay on a foil-lined baking sheet and bake in a preheated 225°F. oven for 20 to 30 minutes longer. Cool thoroughly.) Return shell to pie plate. Wrap airtight. Store as for meringue shells.

Per serving—meringues/pie shell (based on 8 servings):
Calories: 100   Grams of fat: 0   Grams of saturated fat: 0
Mgrams cholesterol: 0   Mgrams sodium: 61
Percentage of calories from fat: 0

Per serving—meringues with ¼ cup yogurt and 2 tablespoons berries
Calories: 158   Grams of fat: 1.2   Grams of saturated fat: 0.6
Mgrams cholesterol: 2   Mgrams sodium: 101
Percentage of calories from fat: 7

lemon roulade (rolled lemon sponge cake)

$\mathcal{C}$arefully designed to be easy to handle and roll up without breaking, this fragrant lemon sponge cake is a basic component of several desserts in this book, including Lemon Cake Roll with Lemon Cream (pages 21–22), Apricot Tipsy Parson (pages 93–94), and Charlotte Royale (pages 84–86). $\sim$ Since the only fat in this cake comes from egg yolks, it can fit into even a very low-fat regime.

2 large egg yolks

½ cup granulated sugar, divided

⅛ teaspoon salt

2¼ teaspoons finely grated lemon zest (yellow part of skin)

1¼ teaspoons vanilla extract

⅛ teaspoon almond extract

¼ cup orange juice

½ cup white cake flour (unsifted)

¼ cup cornstarch

1¼ teaspoons baking powder

3 large egg whites, completely free of yolk

About 1 tablespoon powdered sugar, for dusting cake roll

Makes 9 or 10 servings.

Preheat oven to 375° F. Grease a 10- by 15-inch (or similar-size) jelly-roll pan. Line pan with wax paper or baking parchment, allowing paper to overhang pan ends slightly. Grease paper or spray with nonstick spray coating.

In a large mixer bowl, combine yolks with half the sugar, the salt and 1 tablespoon hot tap water. Beat on medium speed until foamy. Raise speed to high and continue beating for 3 to 5 minutes, or until mixture is lightened, increased in volume, and flows in thick ribbons from beaters. Beat in lemon zest, vanilla, almond extract, and orange juice. Sift flour, cornstarch, and baking powder over beaten yolks. Lightly fold ingredients 5 or 6 times with a rubber spatula to partially mix them. Set aside.

In a grease-free mixer bowl with grease-free beaters, beat egg whites on medium speed until frothy. Raise speed to high and beat until *soft peaks just begin to form;* be careful not to overbeat. Immediately begin adding remaining ¼ cup sugar, about a tablespoon at a time, and beat until whites stand in firm but not dry peaks. Using a wire whisk, mix about a third of whites into yolk mixture. Then fold yolk mixture into remaining whites until ingredients are evenly incorporated but not overmixed. Immediately turn out batter into prepared pan, spreading to edges and forming an evenly thick layer.

Quickly transfer to center oven rack. Bake for 7 to 10 minutes, or until cake is just slightly darker at the edges and springs back when lightly pressed in center. Transfer pan to a wire rack. Very loosely drape a slightly damp tea towel over cake and let stand for about 5 minutes. Remove towel. Run a knife around pan edges to loosen cake and paper. Very lightly dust a long sheet of wax paper with powdered sugar. Lift cake and attached paper from pan and lay, cake side down, on wax paper. Gently peel off attached paper and discard. Trim off any dry edges of cake. Cover cake with a fresh sheet of wax paper. Let cake stand for about 10 minutes longer, until cooled to warm.

Turn over cake so original top (browned side) is facing up. Carefully and *tightly* roll up sponge cake *and paper* to form an evenly thick log. (If preparing the Lemon Roll, roll from a short side; if preparing the Charlotte Royale, roll from a long side.) Secure log in wax paper by folding or twisting ends. Tighten wrapping to compress log and keep it from unrolling. Store log in the refrigerator for up to 2 days or wrap airtight and freeze for up to 2 weeks. (Thaw before using.)

Per serving (based on 10 servings):
Calories: 94   Grams of fat: 1.1   Grams of saturated fat: 0.3
Mgrams cholesterol: 43   Mgrams sodium: 92
Percentage of calories from fat: 11

buttery low-cholesterol pastry

*M*y insistence that the pastry always be as good as the rest of the pie created a serious challenge for me in this book: Could I come up with a tender, flavorful, and manageable pie crust while still limiting cholesterol and fat? ∾ The answer is "sort of." The recipe presented here yields pastry that is as tempting and tender as anyone could wish. It also contains markedly less fat and cholesterol than most fine-quality pie crusts—just 8.3 grams of fat and 40 milligrams of cholesterol for an ample—and buttery—single crust. (After much experimentation, I've discovered that the absolute minimum fat needed for desirable texture is 1 tablespoon per ¼ cup flour.) ∾ Still, even this carefully devised, reduced-fat crust is not really low-fat. It is a luxury for fat watchers and must be used judiciously. To this end, I always pair it with an extra-lean filling, which helps lower the overall percentage of fat in a dessert. And I control the amount of pastry, providing just enough but no extra for any individual recipe. (This means that there are no two-crust pies in *Dream Desserts*!)

1⅓ cups all-purpose flour

Scant ½ teaspoon salt

1½ tablespoons well-chilled Browned Butter (page 147) or
    chilled unsalted butter, cut into small pieces

3½ tablespoons canola or safflower oil

1 tablespoon lemon juice combined with 3 tablespoons
    ice water

Makes one 9-inch, 9½-inch deep-dish, or thin 10-inch pastry shell; about 8 servings.

Combine flour and salt in food processor. Process for 10 seconds. Sprinkle butter and oil over flour. Process just until mixture is consistency of coarse crumbs; don't overprocess. If necessary, stop and scrape bowl bottom and sides once or twice. (If processor is unavailable, cut in butter and oil with forks or your fingertips, until mixture is consistency of coarse crumbs.) Turn out mixture into a bowl. Add 2 tablespoons plus 1 teaspoon lemon water, gently mixing with a fork until mixture is moistened and holds together. (It should not be at all dry; if necessary, add a bit more lemon water until it is evenly moistened but not wet.) Knead briefly with your hands until particles are smoothly incorporated. Shape pastry into a smooth disc.

Lay disc between sheets of wax paper. Using a rolling pin and working with a pressing motion, roll into an evenly thick round: Roll into a 12-inch round for a 9-inch shell and a 12½-inch round for 9½-inch deep-dish shell or 10-inch shell; layer will be thin. Check underside of dough while rolling and smooth out any wrinkles that form. Patch any tears as necessary. Peel off one sheet of paper. Lift dough and attached paper and center, dough-side down, over *lightly greased* pie plate. Drape in plate, smoothing into place. Gently peel away wax paper, patching any tears if necessary. (If dough feels soft and warm, refrigerate for about 10 minutes to firm slightly.) Trim dough so edge is even and overhangs plate by ½ inch all around. Fold overhanging pastry into plate all the way around to form a plump edge. Press evenly and adjust

so pastry edge is flush with top edge of plate. Finish edge by fluting with fingers or pressing into edge with tines of a fork. Loosely cover pastry with plastic wrap and refrigerate for at least 15 minutes and up to 8 hours. Bake as directed in individual recipes.

Per serving (based on 8 servings):
Calories: 141   Grams of fat: 8.3   Grams of saturated fat: 1.8
Mgrams cholesterol: 5   Mgrams sodium: 155
Percentage of calories from fat: 53

browned butter

*T*here is no substitute for the taste of butter in fine desserts, but in reduced-fat recipes just a little bit has to go a long way. Fortunately, you can heighten the flavor and aroma of even a small amount of butter by simply simmering it in a saucepan until lightly browned. (The butter is then returned to the refrigerator, and used in place of regular butter as needed.) This technique is used with great success in a number of recipes in *Dream Desserts*, including Vanilla Pound Cake (pages 28–29), Buttery Low-Cholesterol Pastry (pages 146–47), and Fresh Peach Crumb Cake (pages 37–38).

½ **cup (1 stick) unsalted butter**

Makes scant 8 tablespoons.

Melt butter in a medium-sized saucepan over medium heat. Adjust heat so butter boils very gently but steadily. Cook, uncovered and stirring frequently, for 4 to 6 minutes, until foaming subsides and butter turns golden but not brown; watch carefully to avoid

burning on the bottom. Immediately remove pan from heat, stirring for 30 seconds. Set aside to cool slightly. Transfer to a storage container and store in the refrigerator for up to 3 weeks or in the freezer for up to 3 months.

Per serving (based on 8 servings):
Calories: 108   Grams of fat: 12.2   Grams of saturated fat: 7.6
Mgrams cholesterol: 33   Mgrams sodium: 2
Percentage of calories from fat: 99

tart & tartlet pastry (pâte sucrée)

*T*his crisp, faintly sweet tart and tartlet pastry is prepared like a cookie dough and is easy to handle. It is sturdier than regular pie pastry and holds up well even when used with a juicy fruit. ～ If you are preparing a tart shell for a dessert not included in this book, follow the directions for shaping and baking provided here. If the pastry is part of a recipe in *Dream Desserts*, simply prepare the dough and then bake as directed in individual recipes. (To prepare tartlet shells rather than a single tart, follow directions at the end of the recipe.)

2 tablespoons canola or safflower oil

1 tablespoon plus 2 teaspoons Browned Butter (page 147)
    or unsalted butter, cool and firm but not hard

3 tablespoons granulated sugar

1 large egg

Generous ¼ teaspoon finely grated lemon zest (yellow part
    of skin)

1½ teaspoons vanilla extract

2 tablespoons cornstarch

1 cup plus 2 tablespoons all-purpose flour

*Makes one 9- or 10-inch tart shell, about 8 servings;
variation: 8 to 12 tartlet shells, depending on size of pans.*

Preheat oven to 375° F. Lightly grease a 9- or 10-inch fluted tart pan, preferably one with a removable bottom.

In a large mixer bowl with mixer set on medium speed, beat together oil, butter, and sugar until well blended and smooth. In a small bowl or cup, beat egg with a fork until well blended. Measure out 3 tablespoons egg and add to mixer; discard any remaining egg or reserve for another purpose. Add lemon zest, vanilla, and cornstarch to mixer. Beat until ingredients are smoothly incorporated. Beat in flour on low speed just until smoothly incorporated. Shape dough into a ball. Roll out dough into an 11½-inch round between sheets of wax paper. While rolling out, check underside of wax paper several times and smooth out any wrinkles that form. Lay dough with the wax paper on a baking sheet and refrigerate for 15 to 20 minutes, until cool and slightly firmer.

Peel off one sheet of paper. Lift dough and attached paper and center, dough side down, in pan. Carefully peel off second sheet of paper. Press and smooth dough into pan, patching any tears and uneven edges as necessary. Trim off excess dough flush with edge of pan; discard trimmings or, if necessary, use them to build up any thin areas along the fluted edge of the pastry.

To bake: Prick dough all over with a fork. Cover pastry with a large sheet of heavy-duty aluminum foil, firmly smoothing foil over pastry and then folding out over pan edges so pastry is completely encased. Set tart pan on a baking sheet. Bake on center oven rack for 15 minutes. Carefully remove foil from pastry and return shell to oven. Bake for 4 to 6 minutes longer, until tart edges are nicely browned and center bottom is firm to the touch. Set shell and pan aside on a wire rack until cooled. Shell will keep, covered, for up to 36 hours. Fill shell as desired.

Variation: Citrus-Spice Tart and Tartlet Pastry

Increase finely grated lemon zest to ½ teaspoon. Add ½ teaspoon peeled and very finely minced fresh ginger root along with lemon zest.

Variation: Tartlet Shells

Prepare dough as directed. Roll out between wax paper sheets into a 10- by 15-inch rectangle. Peel off one layer of wax paper. To determine tartlet shell size, lay a tartlet pan face down on pastry. Using a paring knife, cut around pan, leaving a margin all around that is equal to the height of the pan sides. Repeat until entire surface of dough has been used. Do not lift off dough rounds. Lightly re-cover dough with wax paper. Transfer dough to a baking sheet. Refrigerate for 20 minutes or until dough is cool and slightly firm.

Lift pastry pieces from wax paper and lay each in a tartlet pan. Press into pans, patching any tears in the dough and trimming dough so that it is flush with pan edges. If more tartlet pans are available, gather and re-roll pastry scraps until all pastry is used.

To bake: Prick each tartlet shell all over with a fork. Cover each shell with a square of aluminum foil, firmly smoothing foil over pastry and then folding out over pan edges so pastry is completely encased. Set tartlet pans on a baking sheet. Bake on center oven rack for 8 minutes for 2½- or 3-inch tartlets and 11 minutes for slightly larger ones. Carefully remove foil from tartlet pans and return pans to oven. Bake for 4 to 6 minutes longer, until edges are nicely browned and center bottoms are firm to the touch. Set pan of tartlet shells aside on wire racks to cool.

Per serving (based on 8 servings):
Calories: 151   Grams of fat: 6.6   Grams of saturated fat: 2
Mgrams cholesterol: 29   Mgrams sodium: 7
Percentage of calories from fat: 40

Per serving (based on 12 tartlet servings):
Calories: 101   Grams of fat: 4.4   Grams of saturated fat: 1.3
Mgrams cholesterol: 19   Mgrams sodium: 5
Percentage of calories from fat: 40

improved italian meringue

*T*his recipe for Italian meringue differs from classic versions in two respects: First, it contains a little less sugar than traditional recipes to accommodate today's taste for less sweet desserts. More importantly, it incorporates several steps to ensure that the meringue is thoroughly cooked and, thus, is completely safe to eat. One step is to carefully warm the whites before beginning to beat them. Another is to promptly add the boiling sugar syrup to the pre-warmed whites so they heat to 160° F. and then stay above 140° F. for 3 minutes, the procedure recommended by food-handling guidelines. (For more information on these guidelines, see page 15.) ⌁ In several of the desserts in this book, Italian meringue substitutes for most of the whipped cream or raw egg whites that would normally be incorporated to fluff up the mixture. It can also serve as a replacement for the old-fashioned uncooked (or merely singed) meringue toppings (such as those blanketing Baked Alaska) that are no longer considered safe.

⅓ cup (about 3 large) egg whites, completely free of yolk

1½ tablespoons light corn syrup

⅔ cup granulated sugar

Pinch of salt

¾ teaspoon vanilla extract

Makes generous 1 quart, 8 to 12 servings.

Place whites in a large grease-free mixer bowl. Set in a larger bowl of very hot tap water and let stand for 10 minutes, stirring occasionally. Combine corn syrup, 3 tablespoons water, and the sugar in a 2-quart saucepan, stirring until well blended. Bring to a simmer over medium-high heat. Cover and boil for 2 minutes to allow steam to wash any sugar from pan sides. Uncover and continue simmering, *without stirring,* for about 1 to 1½ minutes longer or until mixture bubbles loudly and reaches 246° F. to 247° F. on a candy thermometer. (To test for doneness without a candy thermometer, drop a teaspoon of syrup into ice water; when cooked to the correct temperature syrup will form an almost brittle ball that holds its shape when squeezed.) Immediately remove pan from heat.

Transfer mixer bowl to mixer and beat whites on medium speed until very frothy and opaque. Raise speed to high and beat until whites just begin to stand in soft peaks; *be careful not to overbeat.* Meanwhile, return syrup to burner and reheat just to boiling. Beating whites on high speed, *immediately* begin pouring boiling syrup in a thin stream *down bowl sides* (avoid beaters or syrup will stick to them or be thrown onto bowl sides), pouring rapidly enough that all syrup is incorporated in about 15 seconds. Add salt, continuing to beat on high speed until mixture is stiffened, glossy, and cooled to barely warm. Beat in vanilla until evenly incorporated. Use immediately or refrigerate, covered, for up to 1 hour.

brandied orange custard cream

$\mathcal{B}$esides being lower in fat than most pastry creams, this versatile custard cream is also a lot easier to make. After much experimentation, I came up with a quick, thorough way of cooking the custard *and* eliminating any chance of curdling: The egg mixture is simply placed over direct heat and then boiled—yes, boiled!—for 2 minutes. That's it, and *no* curdling. The quantities of flour and cornstarch can be decreased slightly (see end of recipe) to yield a custard sauce that can be used, instead of a Sauce Anglaise, with Chocolate Soufflé (pages 78–79).

1 tablespoon plus 2 teaspoons cornstarch

1 tablespoon plus 1 teaspoon all-purpose flour

¼ cup granulated sugar

¼ teaspoon very finely grated orange zest (orange part of skin)

2 tablespoons cognac or good-quality brandy

1 large egg yolk

⅔ cup skim milk

2 tablespoons heavy (whipping) cream

¼ cup fresh orange juice

¾ teaspoon vanilla extract

Makes generous 1 cup cream or 8 (2-tablespoon) servings.

In a medium saucepan, stir together cornstarch, flour, sugar, and orange zest, until well blended. Whisk in brandy until smoothly incorporated. Whisk in egg yolk, stirring well. Stir in milk and cream. Bring mixture to a *full boil* over medium heat, stirring. Boil, stirring, 2 minutes; remove from heat. Stir orange juice and vanilla into egg mixture. Press through a sieve into a storage container. Cover and refrigerate for at least 45 minutes and up to 48 hours before serving. Whisk well before serving.

Variation: Brandied Orange Custard Sauce

Decrease cornstarch to 2¾ teaspoons and flour to 2 teaspoons. Proceed as directed. If sauce becomes too thick when chilled, thin it with a little orange juice before serving.

reduced-fat graham cracker pie & tart shell

$\mathcal{B}$utter or margarine is the ingredient that usually binds graham cracker crumbs into a pie crust, and a standard shell made with 1½ cups crumbs normally calls for about 5 tablespoons of added fat. In this case, only 1 tablespoon each of butter and oil are required and the rest of the fat is replaced by a combination of corn syrup and water. This mixture does the job just as well but yields a much leaner crust. The corn syrup even adds crispness just as fat does. ⌒ This recipe can be substituted whenever a traditional graham cracker pie or tart shell is called for. It can also be paired with the Chocolate Pudding (pages 81–82) to create an easy chocolate pie, or used in the Summer Fruit and Custard Tart (page 53).

Generous 1½ cups graham cracker crumbs
1 tablespoon chilled unsalted butter
1 tablespoon canola or safflower oil
1 tablespoon light corn syrup

Makes one 9½-inch deep-dish pie shell, one 10-inch pie shell, or one 9- or 10-inch tart shell; about 8 servings.

Preheat oven to 375°F. Generously spray a 9½-inch deep-dish pie plate or 10-inch pie plate, or a 9- or 10-inch tart pan with nonstick spray coating.

In a food processor, combine crumbs, butter, and oil. In a small cup, stir together corn syrup and 1 tablespoon water, until well blended. Add corn syrup mixture to processor. Process until mixture is well blended and begins to hold together. Add a few more drops water if mixture is too dry.

(Alternatively, if no processor is available, cut butter and oil into crumbs with a pastry blender or your fingertips. Stir together corn syrup and water and add to mixture. Continue mixing until ingredients are well blended and begin to hold together; add a few drops more water if mixture is too dry.)

Press crumbs smoothly into pan bottom and up sides. If crumbs stick to hands, lay a sheet of wax paper over surface and then press down. Bake for 6 to 9 minutes, until lightly tinged with brown and firm to the touch. Let stand on wire rack until thoroughly cooled. Shell may be used immediately or covered and stored at room temperature for several days, if desired.

Per serving (based on 8 servings):
Calories: 119   Grams of fat: 4.7   Grams of saturated fat: 1.4
Mgrams cholesterol: 4   Mgrams sodium: 101
Percentage of calories from fat: 37

conversion chart

OVEN TEMPERATURES

In the recipes in this book, only Fahrenheit temperatures have been given. Consult this chart for the Centigrade and gas mark equivalents.

Oven	°F	°C	Gas Mark
very cool	250–275	130–140	½–1
cool	300	150	2
warm	325	170	3
moderate	350	180	4
moderately hot	375	190	5
	400	200	6
hot	425	220	7
very hot	450	230	8
	475	250	9

BUTTER

Some confusion may arise over the measuring of butter and other hard fats. In the United States, butter is generally sold in one-pound packages, which contain four equal "sticks." The wrapper on each stick is marked to show tablespoons, so the cook can cut the stick according to the quantity required. The equivalent weights are:

    1 stick = 115 g/4 oz
    1 tablespoon = 15 g/½ oz

EGGS

American eggs are graded slightly differently than British eggs. Here are the equivalent sizes:

    extra large egg (64 g) = size 2 (65 g)
    large egg (57 g) = size 3 (60 g) or 4 (55 g)
    medium egg (50 g) = size 5 (50 g)

FLOUR

American all-purpose flour is milled from a mixture of hard and soft wheats, whereas British plain flour is made mainly from soft wheat. To achieve a near equivalent to American all-purpose flour, use half British plain flour and half strong bread flour.

American cake flour is made from soft wheat and can be replaced by British plain flour alone.

SUGAR

American granulated sugar is finer than British granulated; in fact, it is closer to British caster sugar. British cooks should use caster sugar throughout.

YEAST AND GELATIN

Quantities of dried yeast (called active dry yeast in the United States) are usually given in numbers of packages. Each of these packages contains 7 g/¼ oz of yeast, which is equivalent to a scant tablespoon.

Quantities of unflavored powdered gelatin are usually given in envelopes, each of which contains 7 g/¼ oz (about 1 tablespoon).

INGREDIENTS AND EQUIPMENT GLOSSARY

Although the following ingredients and equipment have different names on opposite sides of the Atlantic, they are otherwise the same or interchangeable.

American	British
baking soda	bicarbonate of soda
bittersweet chocolate	bitter chocolate
broiler/to broil	grill/to grill

American	British
canola oil	use safflower oil
cheesecloth	muslin
confectioners' sugar	icing sugar
cookie cutter	biscuit or pastry cutter
cookie sheet	baking sheet
cornstarch	cornflower
corn syrup	not equivalent, but golden syrup can be used
half-and-half	single cream
heavy cream (37.6% fat)	double cream (35–40% fat)
kitchen towel	tea towel
pancake	griddle cake
low-fat milk	semi-skimmed milk
muffin tin	deep bun tin
parchment paper	nonstick baking paper
semisweet chocolate	plain chocolate
skillet	frying pan
superfine	use caster sugar
unsweetened chocolate	bitter *chocolat pâtissier*
vanilla bean	vanilla pod
whole milk	homogenized milk

VOLUME EQUIVALENTS

These are not exact equivalents for the American cups and spoons, but have been rounded up or down slightly to make measuring easier.

American Measures	Metric	Imperial
¼ t	1.25 ml	
½ t	2.5 ml	
1 t	5 ml	
½ T (1½ t)	7.5 ml	
1 T (3 t)	15 ml	
¼ cup (4 T)	60 ml	2 fl oz
⅓ cup (5 T)	75 ml	2½ fl oz
½ cup (8 T)	125 ml	4 fl oz
⅔ cup (10 T)	150 ml	5 fl oz (¼ pint)
¾ cup (12 T)	175 ml	6 fl oz
1 cup (16 T)	250 ml	8 fl oz
1¼ cups	300 ml	10 fl oz (½ pint)
1½ cups	350 ml	12 fl oz
1 pint (2 cups)	500 ml	16 fl oz
1 quart (4 cups)	1 litre	1¾ pints

WEIGHT EQUIVALENTS

The metric weights given in this chart are not exact equivalents, but have been rounded up or down slightly to make measuring easier.

Avoirdupois	Metric
¼ oz	7 g
½ oz	15 g
1 oz	30 g
2 oz	60 g
3 oz	90 g
4 oz	115 g
5 oz	150 g
6 oz	175 g
7 oz	200 g
8 oz (½ lb)	225 g
9 oz	250 g
10 oz	300 g
11 oz	325 g
12 oz	350 g
13 oz	375 g
14 oz	400 g
15 oz	425 g
1 lb	450 g
1 lb 2 oz	500 g
1½ lb	750 g
2 lb	900 g
2¼ lb	1 kg
3 lb	1.4 kg
4 lb	1.8 kg
4½ lb	2 kg

index

Quality notecards featuring recipes and photographs from *Dream Desserts* are available. Please contact:

Galison Books
36 West 44th Street
New York, New York 10036
(212) 354-8840

Design by Amanda Wilson

Composed in Cochin and Kuenstler Script with QuarkXpress 3.1
on a Macintosh IIsi at Stewart, Tabori & Chang, New York.
Output on a Linotronic L300 at Typogram,
New York, New York.

Printed and bound by Toppan Printing Company, Ltd.,
Tokyo, Japan.